A.W. TOZER

Compiled and Edited by James L. Snyder

THE
DANGERS
OF A
SHALLOW
FAITH

AWAKENING FROM SPIRITUAL LETHARGY

Regal

For more information and
special offers from Regal Books, email us at
subscribe@regalbooks.com

Published by Regal
From Gospel Light
Ventura, California, U.S.A.
www.regalbooks.com
Printed in the U.S.A.

All Scripture quotation are taken from
the *King James Version*. Authorized King James Version.

Library of Congress Cataloging-in-Publication Data
Tozer, A. W. (Aiden Wilson), 1897-1963.
The dangers of a shallow faith : awakening from spiritual lethargy / A.W. Tozer ;
compiled and edited by James L. Snyder.
p. cm.
Includes bibliographical references and index.
ISBN 978-0-8307-6204-0 (trade paper : alk. paper)
1. United States—Church history—20th century. 2. Church renewal—
United States. 3. Revivals—United States. 4. Religious awakening—Christianity.
I. Snyder, James L. II. Title.
BR525.T69 2012
269—dc23
2012003610

Rights for publishing this book outside the U.S.A. or in non-English languages are
administered by Gospel Light Worldwide, an international not-for-profit ministry.
For additional information, please visit www.glww.org, email info@glww.org, or write
to Gospel Light Worldwide, 1957 Eastman Avenue, Ventura, CA 93003, U.S.A.

To order copies of this book and other Regal products in bulk quantities,
please contact us at 1-800-446-7735.

CONTENTS

FOREWORD

The message from A. W. Tozer that you are about to read is one that so many in today's Church need to hear. God has called us in to a deep walk with Him, but many of us are just touching the surface. Not only does this book identify some of the issues that may be limiting our life in Christ, but it also encourages us to know God more fully. The truth of Tozer's words will encourage us to not be comfortable with our current understanding of God. There is a fire that God wants to ignite and rekindle in us to search out the mystery of His will (see Eph. 3:9), which He has promised to reveal to those who seek Him.

Every time I ordain a minister or pastor to plant churches, I read these words that A. W. Tozer prayed on his ordination day:

> *I am Thy servant to do Thy will, and that will is sweeter to me than position or riches or fame and I choose it above all things on earth or in heaven. Though I am chosen of Thee and honored by a high and holy calling, let me never forget that I am but a man of dust and ashes, a man with all the natural faults and passions that plague the race of men. I pray Thee therefore, my Lord and Redeemer, save me from myself and from all the injuries I may do myself while trying to be a blessing to others. Fill me with thy power by the Holy Spirit, and I will go in Thy strength and tell of Thy righteousness, even Thine only. I will spread abroad the message of redeeming love while my normal powers endure.*

Even this small portion of Tozer's prayer expresses the humility with which he approached his calling. There is no greater

5

tone to set a venturing out in ministry than the sober yet faith-filled depths of Tozer. Very few men of God in history have been able to so explore the depths of God while enjoying the heights of His love.

Tozer's writings, however, are not only for ministers. I would recommend this book to anyone who has a heart after God. Reverend James Snyder has done a masterful job of compiling these works to clearly express the depths and heights of Tozer's writings, and I am thankful that he has put these works into a form that can be preserved for generations to come. These are words that shouldn't be lost in the archives of history but should continue to declare the relevant truth in our contemporary Church.

I pray that you will be blessed and challenged to grasp the very depths of Christ as you read this book.

With you in Christ,

Pastor Gary Wilkerson
President, World Challenge, Inc.
Lead Pastor, The Springs Church in Colorado Springs, Colorado

A TRUE PROPHET OF THE CHURCH

Throughout history, the Church has been inundated with self-proclaimed prophets. Whenever I hear of such people, I can't help but think of God's command to the Israelites in Deuteronomy 18:22: "When a prophet speaketh in the name of the LORD, if the thing follow not, nor come to pass, that is the thing which the LORD hath not spoken, but the prophet hath spoken it presumptuously: thou shalt not be afraid of him."

It is a dangerous thing for someone to claim to be a prophet. Of all the ministries set forth in Scripture, it is easiest to discern when a person is not speaking a true prophetic word from God. Perhaps Paul had this in mind when he wrote, "Let the prophets speak two or three, and let the other judge. If any thing be revealed to another that sitteth by, let the first hold his peace. For ye may all prophesy one by one, that all may learn, and all may be comforted. And the spirits of the prophets are subject to the prophets. For God is not the author of confusion, but of peace, as in all churches of the saints" (1 Cor. 14:29-33).

Unfortunately, today it seems that many in the Church will accept *any* person who calls himself or herself a prophet. They hang on the individual's every word, regardless of whether what he or she says ever materializes. It is the oratory of the moment that matters. The prophets we find in Scripture, however, spoke words that actually came to pass. In the Old Testament, the prophets told of things to come; while in the New Testament they served as a form of troubleshooter for the Church, pointing out errors and heresies and then offering the solution in a way that pointed the group of believers back to Christ. They saw clearly, spoke sharply, and were rarely if ever appreciated for it. As Jesus said so eloquently, "A prophet is not without honour, save in his own country, and in his own house" (Matt. 13:57).

When it comes to this kind of a prophet, A. W. Tozer stands out among the rest. He begins this book by stating that he will "go out on a limb a little bit and prophesy." He relates that he can envision a time coming when those in the Church will desert evangelicalism—a time when "the house will be left desolate and there will not be a man of God, a man in whom the Holy Spirit dwells, left among them." It is safe to say that we have lived to see the beginning of this prophecy being fulfilled. And, unfortunately, like the true prophets of old, the evangelical church has heard Tozer but not listened to him.

Tozer's criticism of the Church was never based on malice but rather on a deep love for the body of believers in Jesus Christ. He had a long view of the Church that was deeply rooted in biblical truth—a truth that does not change over time—and he understood that many of the problems the Church were facing were ones his forefathers had faced several generations back. The old preacher in Ecclesiastes was right when he said, "The thing that hath been, it is that which shall be; and that which is done is that which shall be done: and there is no new thing under the sun" (Eccles. 1:9).

For this reason, when Tozer saw things developing within a congregation that he believed was detrimental to its spiritual development, he got riled up and spoke out boldly against it. Yet he also always pointed the way out. He called the danger for what it was and then offered the group he was criticizing a biblical solution that was focused on Christ. In this book, the center of the danger that Tozer perceived was a shallow faith that led to spiritual lethargy. This spiritual condition made the Church vulnerable to an onslaught from the enemy.

The remedy Tozer proposed was as drastic as the spiritual condition of the Church warranted. One item he emphasized was the fact that the world was too much with Christians, and that believers needed to be separated from it. This idea of separation from the world is one that has been lost on this generation of Christians. The Church is so intertwined with the world around that the two are essentially one and the same. However, Tozer recognized that unless believers are separated from the world, they will succumb to spiritual lethargy.

Tozer could not accept a juvenile attitude among believers in the Church. He could not tolerate Christians who became easily bored and looked around for entertainment to relieve that sense of boredom. For Tozer, entertainment was simply the Church synchronizing with the world and succumbing to it. It was utter nonsense to him that the Church wanted to bring itself "up to speed" with the world around it. A worldly church was, in Tozer's thinking, an oxymoron and completely anathema.

As you read this book, you will find that the problems Tozer pointed out in his day are still occurring today. We can truthfully say that the Church has been down this path before! For some reason, each generation of Christians believes they need to reinvent the spiritual wheel, but Tozer was able to see above and beyond all of this because his focus was not on the passing trends. He knew that trends come and go, and that once people acclimate to one trend it is passé, and a new one is around the corner. Like the prophets in Scripture, he saw clearly and spoke sharply, and his assessment of the Church was right on in his time—and still is today.

This book is not just a book of negatives, although it has its fair share. However, in the midst of all of the negative there is positive hope for the soul thirsty for God.

Rev. James L. Snyder

PART I

....

THE DANGERS FACING THE EVANGELICAL CHURCH

1

AT THE BRINK
OF APOSTASY

Having a form of godliness, but denying the power thereof: from such
turn away. For of this sort are they which creep into houses, and lead
captive silly women laden with sins, led away with divers lusts, ever
learning, and never able to come to the knowledge of the truth.

2 TIMOTHY 3:5-7

The evangelical church in America is facing some serious hazards that threaten to bring it to the brink of apostasy. My prayer is that it is not too late for an awakening that will lead to successful reformation.

My use of the term "evangelical" includes all churches that are fundamental, full Gospel, holiness, Anabaptist and Pentecostal—all evangelical churches that believe the Bible and proclaim Jesus Christ to be the only Savior of the world. I have nothing to say to any other church.

It is amazing to me how divided is the evangelical church in America, which reminds me of my mother's old-fashioned apple pie. No matter how thin you slice the pie, every slice believes it is better than the rest of the pie. Even though the "pie" includes the same ingredients, goes through the same process and bakes in the same oven, each piece feels superior to the other piece.

A stanza of the hymn "Onward, Christian Soldiers" by Sabine Baring-Gould (1834–1924) says it as it ought to be:

Like a mighty army
Moves the Church of God;
Brothers, we are treading
Where the Saints have trod;
We are not divided,
All one body we,
One in hope and doctrine,
One in charity.

The meaning of the words in this hymn is where God would have us stand as His Church in this generation.

Let me go out on a limb a little bit and prophesy. I see the time coming when all the holy men whose eyes have been opened by the Holy Spirit will desert worldly evangelicalism, one by one. The house will be left desolate and there will not be a man of God, a man in whom the Holy Spirit dwells, left among them.

The Curse of Worldliness

I hear Jesus saying, "O Jerusalem, Jerusalem, thou that killest the prophets, and stonest them which are sent unto thee, how often would I have gathered thy children together, even as a hen gathereth her chickens under her wings, and ye would not!" (Matt. 23:37). As the Church stands now, the man who sees this condition of worldly evangelicalism is written off as being somewhat fanatical. But the day is coming when the house will be left desolate and there will not be a man of God left among them.

I would like to live long enough to watch this develop and see how things turn out. I would like to live to see the time when the men and women of God—holy, separated and spiritually enlightened—walk out of the evangelical church and form a group of their own; when they get off the sinking ship and let

14

her go down in the brackish waters of worldliness and form a new ark to ride out the storm.

The Bible has no compromise whatsoever with the world. The Bible has a message for the evangelical church, calling it back home. The Bible always sends us out into the world, but never to compromise with the world; and never to walk in the way of the world, but only to save as many as we can. That is the one direction.

So, my Christian friend, if you are settling back, snuggling into your foam rubber chair and resting in your faith in John 3:16 and the fact that you have accepted Jesus Christ, you had better watch yourself. Take heed, lest you also be found wanting. Take heed of your own heart, lest when all is said and done, you have become tied in with the world.

In looking back over the history of Israel in the Old Testament, I cannot help but note that just about every third generation had to throw out all the previous generation's religious accouterments and get back to the original. It started with the Fathers who established their nation upon the clear Word of the Lord. The sons of the Fathers began taking that foundation for granted, adding nonessential elements while allowing crucial and fundamental essentials to slide. In the grandsons, we find a complete disregard for the grandfathers who established Israel, completely disenfranchising the entire nation of Israel from its foundation and completely disregarding the prophets' warning: "Remove not the ancient landmark, which thy fathers have set" (Prov. 22:28).

They sought other gods that suited their fancy at the time. They looked with envy at the nations around them and began adopting the pagan gods of their neighbors. Soon they also adopted the culture of the nations around them, and it was difficult to tell the difference between an Israelite and a Philistine.

Then came the next generation, weary of the religious clap-trap accumulated over the generations. They looked around for something original; invariably, they would stumble upon the Word of the Lord, and in a desperate move, they would clear away all of the religious paraphernalia that had been a part of the previous generation. That which was once mighty and dynamic was returned to with a great deal of anticipation by the younger generation. Today we would call it an awakening or a revival. A true revival or awakening leads to drastic reformation.

It is often the younger generation that sees through the maze of deception and corruption and longs for something original, something with substance. Not only was this true of ancient Israel, but it is also true of the Church. Church history reveals this pattern in almost every generation. When there was a move of God among a group of people, they became so plagued with holy desire that movements—we call them revivals or awakenings—began sweeping men and women into the kingdom of God.

I could point to the Waldensians, who sparked a movement in the Middle Ages; Martin Luther and the great Reformation movement of the 1500s; John and Charles Wesley, in the 1700s. Out of their fiery passion for God came a great movement known as the Methodists, which saved England from a national disaster. These great movements were not only owned by God but were surely started by God, who found hearts hungry for something only God could provide. It would be hard to fathom how many people were actually brought into the kingdom of God through these movements aflame with holy passion for God.

The pattern started with the Fathers of the Church. The sons then came along and tried to keep the movement going, tried to keep the fire burning and make sure they were replicating everything their Fathers did. It only lasted a generation, and then the following generation came along and found themselves burdened with religious bric-a-brac that had absolutely no association with their spiritual roots. "Why do we do this? Why don't we do that?" Soon the grandsons were allowing the world around them to bleed into their fellowship; and before long, there was no visible difference between the Church and the world. The culture of the world had effectively taken over the Church.

Sure, the grandsons looked like their grandfathers. Some of them even spoke in the religious dialect of their grandfathers. For all practical purposes, they were the grandsons carrying on the work of the grandfathers. However, they were not their grandfathers. That which was vital to the grandfathers became incidental to the grandsons. Instead of their religion carrying them forward in holy passion, they were trying to carry their religion, and the weight of it brought them to points of weariness and religious fatigue and final collapse. They sought relief out in the world in the form of compromise. To negotiate with the world is to forfeit the sense of God's presence.

I would estimate that no denomination has ever survived its 100-year anniversary without a drastic overhaul from the inside out. The apostle Paul warns about having "a form of godliness, but denying the power thereof" (2 Tim. 3:5). He adds with an air of finality, "from such turn away."

When a generation comes along dissatisfied with the status quo and has a hunger for God that cannot be quenched by ritual and tradition, most of these do not come out of the religious hierarchy, but come stomping in unceremoniously with such a passion for God that they upset everything they come in contact with and bypass religious protocol, much to the affront of the religious Pharisees and scribes in control at the time. The religious leaders condemn them and try to put them out of "the Church." However, they are the Church, and they in-flame a new generation with a holy passion for the person of God that cannot be quenched.

This is where the evangelical church of our generation is. We are facing such jeopardy; and for the most part, nobody is enumerating those dangers. I want to share a little bit of my insight into this, and perhaps my meager efforts can stir up within the hearts of a new generation a longing and passion for that reality which only comes from an intimate and personal relationship with God through the Lord Jesus Christ.

As I look at the evangelical church today, I see several issues that need to be addressed. The first issue is the spirit of Babylon.

The Haunting Spirit of Babylon

I believe the spirit of Babylon is invading the Church today to the point of controlling it. Anyone who has read the Old Testament understands the significance of the term "Babylon." If you do not know much about this, let me point out the characteristics associated with the spirit of Babylon.

The Spirit of Entertainment

This spirit of Babylon, in the form of entertainment, has not only seeped into the Church but has also been welcomed through the front door with inviting arms and has come in like a flood. It seems so incongruent to me that a generation of Christians should so loathe the accomplishments of their forefathers and the sacrifice associated with the faith once delivered that they would court the frivolous attitude and spirit of "entertainmentism." We are not worshiping God on the throne but have come to the point of worshiping the shadow of the throne.

The average Christian today is addicted to exterior pleasures. Can any Christian church survive today without a heavy dose of entertainment? It is the culture of fun, fun and more fun. Performance has replaced worship. We no longer have worshipers but rather observers and spectators who sit in awe of the performance. The demand is for something that will make us feel good about ourselves and make us forget about all of our troubles.

The Church Fathers were fanatic worshipers, and their worship carried with it a heavy cost, which incidentally, they gladly and eagerly paid. The grandsons are now observers with an appetite for entertainment that has gone wild. They are addicted, with an insatiable appetite, to have one thrill followed by an even bigger thrill. They are as fanatic about entertainment as their fathers were about worship, which explains the difference.

To confuse the matter and make it even worse, we have now what I shall call a performance-oriented worship. Just because you tack the word "worship" onto a phrase does not mean that it is worship acceptable to God. We dance before God, wearing our silly little costumes and doing our silly little jingles, thinking that this in some way impresses the God Almighty, Creator of the heavens and the earth.

The Church Fathers came into the presence of God with a sense of overwhelming reverence, which captivated them and brought them before God in holy silence. What has happened to reverence today? Where are those who get caught up in the spirit of reverence before their God? Where are those who have experienced the holy hush in the presence of God?

Then we have celebrities who are leading our so-called worship today. This mirrors the culture around us. To be a leader in the Church, a man does not have to have spiritual qualifications as much as a personality and a celebrity status. The converted football player wields more influence in churches today than the man who is before God on his knees with a broken heart for his community. Celebrities are now leading us, but they are not leading us down the same pathway the Fathers of the Church established.

The Spirit of Lethargy

All of this has successfully created in today's evangelical church a condition of spiritual lethargy. Because the word "lethargy" is not in common use, I probably need to outline a little bit of what I mean.

By lethargy, I mean living on yesterday's momentum. That seems to explain the condition today. The Church Fathers did not look back and try to live in the past. The Church Fathers looked back to find their compass so they could go forward in the power and demonstration of the Holy Spirit.

If we do not know where we have been, how in the world are we going to determine where we are going? That is the only reason for looking back. We do not look back in order to go back. Rather, we look back so that we can make sure we are going forward in the right direction.

The Spirit of Ease

Too many in the Church today are living on yesterday's momentum. They feel that all of the battles have been fought. They assume that all the struggles in the Church are over. They are the privileged generation that goes to heaven on flowery beds of ease.

Probably the most discouraging aspect of this is that many have grown accustomed to a static condition and have succumbed to a spirit of non-expectation. The only expectation most have is that when they die they fully expect to go to heaven. Apart from that, they are going to spend their time having fun and enjoying their religion.

The Church Fathers did not enjoy their religion. *Foxe's Book of Martyrs* shows what their religion cost them. They did not expect an easy time of it. It was Charles Wesley (1707–1788) in his marvelous hymn "Soldiers of Christ, Arise" that set the tone for his generation:

Soldiers of Christ, arise
And put your armor on,
Strong in the strength which God supplies,
Through His eternal Son.
Strong in the Lord of Hosts,
And in That mighty power,
Who in the strength of Jesus trusts
Is more than a conqueror.

Where are these "soldiers of Christ" today? Where are those who go forth in the "strength which God supplies"? Where are those who are willing to go forth conquering and to conquer?

The tragedy of this generation of Christians is that men have crept in unawares, as prophesied by Paul in the book of Romans, and by Jude in his epistle. We have lowered our guard, and these false prophets have so positioned themselves that they are controlling the destiny of this generation's Christian Church.

Overtaken by Spiritually Impotent Theologians

Another tragedy I associate with today's evangelical church is the fact that we have been overtaken and held hostage by spiritually impotent theologians. I love the word "theology." It simply means the study of God; and there is nothing greater to pursue in this world. Our hearts hunger for God, asking when shall we come and stand before Him?

Then, from the word "theology" comes the word "theologian." It used to mean a person who has specialized in the study of God, but it has come to mean someone who is an expert in a slice of Christianity. In many cases that slice is rather small and disassociated from the whole.

These contemporary theologians deal with doctrinal minutia. Their expertise is in the area of rethinking doctrinal positions in light of contemporary society and culture. For some reason, they believe that because society has changed so drastically, our doctrinal positions need to change accordingly. To reexamine the doctrine of the inspiration of Scripture, for example, is an exercise in futility.

By slicing and dicing doctrinal positions, we have come to a point of not knowing what we believe. Not only that, but we also need new translations of the Scripture. I am not against that at all. Every time a new translation is published, I am one of the first to purchase it.

However, a new, updated translation of the Scripture is not the answer. It is amazing that in a generation of Christians with more modern translations of the Scriptures than all the other generations put together, it is just about the weakest group of Christians we have ever seen.

It is not by reading the Scriptures in the original languages or in some contemporary version that makes us better Christians. Rather, it is getting on our knees with the Scriptures spread before us, and allowing the Spirit of God to break our hearts. Then, when we have been thoroughly broken before God Almighty, we get up off our knees, go out into the world and proclaim the glorious message of Jesus Christ, the Savior of the world.

Experts who know everything but what is essential in the spiritual life are now running our churches. What I want to know is what are they expert in? It does not seem that many of them are expert in knowing God as the Fathers knew God. They do not seem to have that overwhelming awe that was predominant in the Early Church movement. What have our experts done for the Church except to push it into a rut, allowing the letter of the law to dominate and control while denying the power of the Holy Spirit? I fear that we may have become too apologetic with our apologetics, and in trying to please everyone we end up destroying the truth.

This has created a religious class system. All these learned doctors with their PhDs and their noses firmly pointed north have caused great strife in the Church of Jesus Christ. Don't they know that the devil is a better theologian than all of us put together? The Scriptures tell us that the devil even trembles before God, but he has no part in God's kingdom: "Thou believest that there is one God; thou doest well: the devils also believe, and tremble" (Jas. 2:19).

This only shows the tyranny of religion today. In the Early Church, everybody was part of the ministry team. Everybody was expected to go out into the world and preach the glorious redeeming message of Jesus Christ. Certainly, there were categories—such as elders and bishops and apostles. The Church ran quite efficiently by all Christians working together, each of them knowing where they belonged, and doing their part.

Now we have teams of experts who only know the letter of the law. We have people who have become religious snobs putting on a show for Christians in the hopes that the Sunday offering would be more than sufficient to subsidize a lifestyle of greed. It is not hard to see that a spirit of Babylon creating a condition of spiritual lethargy has invaded today's Church—all of this orchestrated by spiritually impotent theologians.

To minimize the danger is to jeopardize an entire generation of Christians. This is the curse of apostasy. Apostasy starts when certain men creep in unawares and replace the Holy Spirit as the guiding force of the Christian movement. The Church was never designed to be piloted by men; rather, the Holy Spirit birthed the Church on the day of Pentecost as a vehicle through which He could do His work in each generation.

Let us face the dangers by realizing just how serious the situation is. Then, in the power and demonstration of the Holy Spirit, let us break down all of these artificial divisions and all of the impotent hierarchy that denominationalism has developed. Let us get back to the kind of Christianity that was birthed on the day of Pentecost and "be not entangled again with the yoke of bondage" (Gal. 5:1).

Must Jesus Bear the Cross Alone
Thomas Shepherd (1665–1739)

Must Jesus bear the cross alone
And all the world go free?
No, there's a cross for everyone
And there's a cross for me.

How happy are the saints above
Who once went sorrowing here!
But now they taste unmingled love
And joy without a tear.

The consecrated cross I'll bear
Till death shall set me free
And then go home my crown to wear
For there's a crown for me.

Upon the crystal pavement down
At Jesus' pierced feet
Joyful I'll cast my golden crown
And His dear Name repeat.

O precious cross! O glorious crown!
O resurrection day!
When Christ the Lord from Heav'n comes down
And bears my soul away.

2

SEEKING A SUBSTITUTE FOR GOD

By the rivers of Babylon, there we sat down, yea, we wept, when we
remembered Zion. We hanged our harps upon the willows in
the midst thereof. For there they that carried us away captive
required of us a song; and they that wasted us required of us mirth,
saying, Sing us one of the songs of Zion.
How shall we sing the LORD's song in a strange land?

PSALM 137:1-4

Moses—who was up on Mount Sinai meeting God and receiving the Ten Commandments—did not realize that down below God's people were in danger. Caught up in the presence of God, Moses had no other thought but God. Down below, it was a different story.

While Moses was on the mountaintop, his brother, Aaron, succumbed to Israel's attitude of boredom. Moses had been away longer than anticipated, and something was needed to titillate the carnal appetites of God's people. Frankly, they had grown tired of waiting on Moses.

When you look at the facts, it is easy to see that one of the great dangers facing God's people is in this area of religious boredom. Boredom with religion is conceivable, but being bored with God is not. Those who have encountered God and His mighty, awesome presence could never come to the point of boredom. Religion, however, with all of its tiresome dos and don'ts, sets us up for such boredom. Anyone who tries to follow his religion religiously experiences great moments of boredom in the minutia.

Israel had experienced all the marvelous miracles of God on their behalf, yet they grew bored with the God of those miracles. Aaron, when faced with Moses' anger about the situation, said:

> Let not the anger of my lord wax hot: thou knowest the people, that they are set on mischief. For they said unto me, Make us gods, which shall go before us: for as for this Moses, the man that brought us up out of the land of Egypt, we [know] not what is become of him. And I said unto them, Whosoever hath any gold, let them break it off. So they gave it me: then I cast it into the fire, and there came out this calf (Exod. 32:22-24).

The environment of the spirit of Babylon has created a situation where the Church is being dominated by what I shall call cults. These cults have so dominated today's Christian scene that true Christianity has a hard time even breathing. Let me break it down and show you what I mean.

The Cult of Imitation

The first cult dominating Christianity today is to imitate what we see outside of the Church. This is a characteristic of immaturity, like a little toddler who sees someone do something and tries to imitate it without knowing what it really means. The secular media in America sets the standards for us in the Church.

Churches now have "programs" directed by "emcees." This is directly from the world of entertainment. This sacred cow of the world has been brought into the sanctuary of the living God. The Church naïvely imitates what it sees in the world without any regard to consequence.

There was a time when the Church set the standard for music. Then the world imitated the Church. Men like Beethoven, Mozart and Handel set the whole world singing, and the focus of their music was the Church. We no longer initiate our music; rather, we pipe in the music of the world around us. Now we go tramping out into the world in order to import into the Church the sounds of the world. We offer this "swine" on the altar of Jehovah. What blasphemy. We have so much more to offer God. Importing the culture around us instead of adoring the nature and character of Christ within us is the sad reality of today's Christian.

Our literature is no different. If there is a best seller out in the world, you can be sure it will be imitated in the Church eventually. Instead of writing great literature that honors God, the Church and the things of heaven, we are duplicating the dreary, morally questionable literature of the world. It seems to be a trophy to some writers to see how close to the edge they can get and not fall over. I have a news bulletin. They are not in danger of falling over the cliff; they have already fallen and do not know it yet.

The reason for this is that Christianity is greatly misunderstood even by those who claim to be Christians. True Christianity is a mystery, a wonder, something alien and transcendent in this world. The Christianity of the New Testament is incomprehensible to the world. There is absolutely no way to build a bridge between the world's standards and the Church's standards.

Some say it is a great honor and a mark of achievement to write a book acceptable both to the world and to the Church. Something is wrong here. I cannot find anything in the Scriptures or even in Church history that in any way suggests compatibility between the world and the Church. The taste of the Church should be infinitely higher and greater than the world's. What satisfies the Church should in no way satisfy the world. The true Christian has an insatiable appetite for Christ and the things of Christ, while the world has no such appetite.

Christ stands alone, and He does not imitate; neither does He court the world in a lame attempt to win the world. Many evangelical churches are closer to the world than to New Testament standards in almost every regard.

The Cult of Entertainment

Related to the cult of imitation is the cult of entertainment. This is probably the most destructive heresy poisoning the evangelical church today. The idea that religion is a form of entertainment is so far removed from New Testament teaching that it amazes me that otherwise good churches have succumbed to it.

Again, this is best seen in modern literature. It has given us a type of religious fiction that is unrealistic, affected and false. The quality of this is so far below New Testament standards and the standards set forth throughout Church history that I am amazed it even sells. Yet this kind of religious entertainment flies off the shelves faster than anything.

What this generation of Christians needs is not religious entertainment to satisfy carnal appetites; rather, it needs some biblically based literature that challenges and stirs the soul to deeper appreciation of God and Christ and the whole plan of salvation. It is true that what we feed is what grows. If we feed the carnal nature and its appetite, that will be the overpowering aspect of our life. If we feed the spiritual, our appetite for the things of God will grow.

The Cult of Celebrity

The third cult dominating the evangelical church today is the cult of celebrity. And right here I should just quit. For some reason the leaders in the evangelical church today believe that in order to accomplish what they want to accomplish for Christ, they need some converted celebrity to lead the way.

This converted celebrity is supposed to do for the evangelical church what the man of God cannot do. After all, the celebrity has an "in" with the world. The people impressed by the converted celebrity are carnal Christians, and only until a bigger celebrity comes along. Where is that generation that fell on their knees before God with broken hearts for the world around them? Where are those men who gave up everything to reach the world of unsaved men and women?

Where are the D. L. Moodys of the Church today? Where are the A. B. Simpsons? Where are the Adoniram Judsons? Where are the J. Hudson Taylors? Where are the Susanna Wesleys? And where are the Lady Julians? And there are many others I could name. The average Christian today is unworthy to loose their shoelaces.

To know of these men and women and the work they did for Christ, and then turn around and go after some converted celebrity to follow, is almost as close to blasphemy as we can possibly get. We swoon over celebrity. Whatever they say, we accept as the important word for the day, even if it goes contrary to plain biblical teaching. St. Ignatius said, "Apart from Him, let nothing dazzle you." We are allowing everything but "Him" to dazzle us these days. We have become rather bored with God and the truths of Scripture. We seem to need something to jazz it all up and excite us. This has taken us far down the road to replacing God.

The Early Church was in wonderment at Christ. He dazzled them and stirred within such feelings of amazement that they could never get over Christ. All they talked about was Christ. All they thought about, from morning to night, was Christ. Christ was their only reason for living, and they were more than willing to die for Him.

Now we look to celebrity to dazzle us. For some reason, we assume that carnal entertainment is the appropriate replacement for the sanctified adoration of the Most High. All of this worldly talent celebrity status is foreign to the New Jerusalem. No cheap thrill can ever replace the ecstatic joy of knowing Jesus Christ.

Israel Overwhelmed by Babylon

While Israel in Babylon did not cease to be Israel, she lost her ability to sing high praise unto Jehovah in worship. Her music was gone. What was natural in Israel prior to Babylon became impossible in Babylon. "How shall we sing the LORD's song in a strange land?" (Ps. 137:4) the Jewish captives wailed as they thought of their Jewish homeland.

The songs of Zion were not forthcoming in the midst of the glories of Babylon. Though Israel had lost her "awe" of Jehovah and had become overwhelmed by Babylon, those who remembered the high praise of Jehovah in Israel lamented. The cheap jingles of Babylon did not compare to the songs of Zion.

In Exodus 32, we find that while Moses was on the mountaintop receiving the commandments from God, Israel was falling into apostasy. They made themselves an idol contrary to the Lord's commandment. Israel proclaimed a feast of dedication and offered their golden calf idol to God in absolute defiance of God's orders. Aaron should have known better, but he went along with the crowd.

Worshiping at the Wrong Altar

Today's evangelical church also has gods they dedicate contrary to God's commandment. With reckless abandon, they worship at the altars of these pagan gods.

The Altar of Marketing

The first worship is at the altar of publicity. Many evangelical Christians feverishly worship publicity marketing as though it were the panacea for all problems. How can they get people to come into their church unless there is a huge publicity campaign? Publicity now is to do what the Holy Spirit did under the Fathers of the Church. Madison Avenue is no replacement for the Holy Spirit moving in the hearts of men and women.

Many Christians worship at the altar of success. Certainly, I believe God wants us to be successful in our Christian walk and in our evangelization of the world. The problem comes in defining success according to the world's terms of success. According to these definitions, Christ would be a complete failure. And the early apostles certainly would have died as failures. Moreover, all through Church history, the great men of God were certainly unsuccessful according to today's definition of success. What the world considers successful, God determines to be an abomination. The successful Christian is one who realizes he is but a pilgrim in this world looking for a city whose builder and foundation is God (see Heb. 11:10; 13:14).

The Altar of Money

Many in today's evangelical church worship at the altar of money. Nobody would disagree with the fact that money is needed to run our missions programs and outreach ministries to our communities and the world. Nobody understood this more than men of great faith like A. B. Simpson, George Müller and J. Hudson Taylor. These men, and many more who followed in their train, prayed in literally millions of dollars to accomplish the work God laid upon their shoulders. However, the difference to them was that money represented a means to accomplish something; whereas, today money is the goal.

The Altar of Activity

The Church also worships at the altar of activity. It almost goes without saying that in today's evangelical church, activity has become a god. Every night of the week there is some activity going on that is absolutely wearing out God's people. When do we have time to stay at home? When do we have time to go to our closets and spend time in prayer and intercession for the community around us? Activity for activity's sake is a great trap in our society. Certainly, we need to go out and get some exercise. Certainly, the Bible condemns the lazy sluggard. But, when activity becomes an end in itself, it becomes an altar at which the Church worships.

I know the reasoning behind some of this. If we do not have activities for our young people, the world will get them. Children today are stimulated to want expensive toys. I can remember the pleasure I took in homemade playthings I constructed out of bits of leftover material. Not only did I have the joy of creation, but I also had the fun of play. No more. We now have an over-stimulated generation. No longer do great feelings rise from within; they must be induced by extravagant saturations from the outside. The world lives by overstimulation, one soul-wrenching episode after another. And the Church is right there with the world. It should be that great thoughts stimulate us to the highest passion our mind and feelings can stand!

The Altar of Pleasure

The most perplexing altar in the evangelical church today is the altar of pleasure. Nobody can read the Bible without coming to the conclusion that God takes great pleasure in His creation and, therefore, pleasure is good, wholesome and godly. The problem comes in what it takes to give us pleasure. Pleasure in and of itself is not wrong; but what it takes to give us that sense of pleasure can be wrong. Do we take pleasure in the work of God? Do we take pleasure in the fellowship of God's people? Do we take pleasure in the presence of God? Or must we go outside the circumference of our Christian fellowship and find pleasure out in the world? This is wrong.

The worst part is that we have incorporated into Church the activities and pleasures of the world. Whatever is stimulating to the average person out in the world is soon integrated into the program of the local church. Find any pleasure out in the world and you will eventually see it in the evangelical church. How in the world has the Church arrived at this point?

It all begins by ascribing false value to things and then assuming the soundness of those values. Following that comes the use of poetry, music, drama and literature to authenticate those values. It is all based upon the assumed soundness of those values while denying and ignoring any evidence of the falsity of those values.

What we must remember is that only he who takes orders from Jesus Christ belongs to Him. The evangelical church is in the process of compromising this very thing and ignoring "thus saith the Lord." Yes, we want any benefits that Christ may confer upon us. We want His help, protection and guidance. We even get misty-eyed over His birth, life, death, teaching and example. The problem comes when we will not take orders from Him. Christ cannot save the one He cannot control. To claim to be saved while ignoring His commandments is to live in utter delusion.

All is not lost, however. Help is available. An awakening is possible. In one flash of spiritual intelligence, God can make a man or woman know, in the deepest meaning of the word, more that matters to his soul for eternity than can be learned in 10 years of hard study. Yet it is also true that long meditation on divine truth and the habit of obedience to such truths as are known are the necessary conditions before such a divine flash is given. The Holy Spirit will not illuminate an irresponsible soul; or if once, then never again. He requires that we live in accord with our higher privileges.

Would You Live for Jesus?
Cyrus S. Nusbaum (1861–1937)

Would you live for Jesus, and be always pure and good?
Would you walk with Him within the narrow road?
Would you have Him bear your burden, carry all your load?
Let Him have His way with thee.

Would you have Him make you free, and follow at His call?
Would you know the peace that comes by giving all?
Would you have Him save you, so that you can never fall?
Let Him have His way with thee.

Would you in His kingdom find a place of constant rest?
Would you prove Him true in providential test?
Would you in His service labor always at your best?
Let Him have His way with thee.

His power can make you what you ought to be;
His blood can cleanse your heart and make you free;
His love can fill your soul, and you will see
'Twas best for Him to have His way with thee.

3

The Platform for False Teaching

Beloved, when I gave all diligence to write unto you of
the common salvation, it was needful for me to write unto you,
and exhort you that ye should earnestly contend for the
faith which was once delivered unto the saints.

JUDE 1:3

The apostle Jude had planned to write an encouraging letter, just as you might sit down to write a letter of encouragement to a friend. He planned to deal with what he called "our common salvation." But an unpleasant circumstance had arisen in the church that forced him to write another kind of letter. Certain men had crept in unnoticed. These men lived evil personal lives and taught doctrine contrary to the Christian faith. They had been foreseen and condemned by the Lord Himself when He was on earth. Jude wrote to challenge the victims of these teachers to contend for the truth—not what they had discovered themselves, but what had been delivered to them by revelation.

Down through the centuries, a platform for false teaching slowly developed within the evangelical church. Such is the nature of this development that few were conscious this was going on. False teaching—teaching that things are other than they actually are—begins with a wrong concept. When we have discovered or had revealed to us the facts about things, both physical and spiritual, we are morally required to acknowledge those facts and make our teaching conform to them.

This is the broad framework upon which everything else must hang—that things are as they are, whether we like it or not. It is our business to find out how they are, accept them as they are and then make our teaching conform to them as they are. That is rather simple, isn't it? Correct doctrine, then, is of vital importance, because it is simply the teaching of things as they are.

We live in a mathematical and a moral world. God runs His physical world with mathematical exactness. He runs His moral world with moral exactness. Nonconformity in either sphere brings sure disaster. False teaching, then, is falsifying data and vital facts. Therefore, telling the truth about things is simply finding out what they are and conforming our words to these facts.

It is so with spiritual truths. When truth has been revealed in the Word of God, our business is to find out what that truth is, and in all of our teaching conform to that truth. We are not to edit or change it, but to let it stand just as it is.

Let an engineer be wrong about a position, and if he builds according to that wrong concept, his building will collapse around him. Let a navigator be wrong about where he is taking his ship, and his ship will run onto a sandbar or a rock and shatter, sinking out of sight. Nonconformity to the truth brings disaster. The enormity of the disaster depends upon the high level or the low level of the facts you have before you.

A Wrong Concept of God

False teaching is the falsifying of data on vital points about God, about ourselves, about sin and about Christ. First, any false teaching must begin with a *wrong concept of God*. No one who holds a right concept of God can go far wrong in anything else. All the mistakes that have been made, all the great fundamental errors, have rested on a wrong concept of God.

Men are not willing to let God be what He says He is. They attempt to change, correct, alter and apologize for God, in an attempt to make Him be other than what He is. God is, and we had better accept Him as He is. God is, and the angels want Him to be what He is. God is, and the elders and the saints and heavenly creatures want Him to be what He is. We had better want Him to be what He is, and conform ourselves to what He is. No lasting structure can be built on a bad foundation. A faulty foundation will cause it to sink, collapse, lean and fall over, bringing the structure down in time.

Of all foundations, God is the most important, because God is God, and He made the heavens and the earth and all the things therein. It would be a great and bitter error for a man or woman to go on for a lifetime believing certain things about God only to learn they were not true. To think they were talking to the God of heaven and earth and find that they were talking to a god fashioned out of their own imagination.

It would be a tragic calamity to the human spirit to pray and preach a lifetime about a god who was not the true God but a composite of ideas drawn from philosophy and psychology and other religions and superstitions. God is what He is, and we had better learn what God is and then conform our teachings to that truth. If we take away any of the attributes of God, we weaken our concept of God.

Some Christians have taken all the justice, judgment and hatred of sin out of the nature of God and have nothing left but a soft god. Others have taken love and grace out and have nothing left but a god of judgment. Or they have taken away the personality of God and have nothing left but a mathematical god—the god of the scientists. All these are false, inadequate conceptions of God.

Our God is a God of justice, grace, righteousness and mercy. While He is a God of mathematical exactness, He is also a God who could take babies in His arms and pat their heads and smile. He is a God who forgives. So we had better make the study of His Word the business of our lives to find out what He is, and then we must conform our views to His.

A Wrong Concept of Ourselves

Any wrong idea of God is bound to give us *a wrong idea of ourselves*. We can know ourselves only as we know God. If our theology is false, our anthropology must be false. If we are wrong about God, we will never know who, what or why we are where we are.

We can only explain ourselves in light of the doctrine that God made man out of the dust of the ground and blew into his nostrils the breath of life, and so man became a living soul. Science has discovered many things about God, but they have not discovered it in context. They have not begun with God and reasoned down to His world. They have begun with the world and tried to reason up to God, but stop short of finding God.

If a man is wrong about God, he is bound to be wrong about himself. If he is wrong about the artist, he will be wrong about the picture. If he is wrong about the potter, he will be wrong about the vessel. If he is wrong about God, he will be wrong about the creature.

While multiplying scientific facts all around, men are wrong because they have left God out and say in their hearts, "There is no God; or if there is a God, He is a God of mathematics and laws, but not the God that the Bible makes Him out to be." That is all wrong, and you cannot know truth about yourself unless you first know truth about God.

You came from the hand of God, and back to God you must go, for judgment or for blessing. Until you take God in and understand God, and let Him be what He claims to be, and believe about you what God says about you, you are believing false doctrine. If you believe you are any better than God says you are, you are in error. If you believe you are any different from what God says you are, you are in error. You have falsified the data, or somebody has falsified the data and made you a victim.

Believe about yourself what God says about you. Believe you are as bad as God says you are, and believe you are as far from Him as God says you are. Then believe in Christ and that you can come as near to Him as He says you can, and accept what He says about you as being true.

A Wrong Concept of Sin

Sin cannot be understood until we believe in God and what He has said about us. Sin is that intrusive, ever-present, ubiquitous phenomenon found in all mankind and manifested in hate, lies, dishonesty, murder, crime and injustice, necessitating law and police and jails and gallows and locks and the grave. There are those who would deny sin, or rename it, and, of course, that is falsifying the data. There are those who would treat it as a disease, but they are falsifying the data.

God said that sin is a breaking of the law, a rebellion against His will. God says that it's a nature inherited from our fathers and mothers. God says that it is an act against the faith and love and mercy of God. God says that it is rebellion against the constituted authority of the Majesty on High. God says it is iniquity, and it is personally chargeable to everyone who commits it. God says, "The soul that sinneth, it shall die" (Ezek. 18:20).

The truth concerning sin always requires that we believe the truth concerning God—that He is sovereign, holy and just. The truth concerning ourselves is that we are His creation, a fallen image of what God intended. Sin, therefore, is a moral rebellion; it is responsible for all evil choices. We had better believe about sin what God says about sin or we will be falsifying the data. Falsified data in spiritual things will bring more terrible consequences than falsifying data in material things.

The doctor who miscounts the number of pills he gives a patient may kill the patient, but that would only destroy the body. The preacher who misjudges or miscounts the truth concerning sin and man and God will damn his hearers, which is infinitely more terrible. Truth concerning God means that we must accept God's sovereignty, His holiness, His justice, His grace, His love and all that the Bible says about God. Concerning ourselves, it requires that we must believe in ourselves as a fallen image of God—ones who once bore His image, but fell.

A Wrong Concept About Christ Himself

If you do not have a right concept of God, of yourself and of sin, you will have a twisted and imperfect concept of Christ. It is my honest and charitable conviction that the Christ of the average religionist today is not the Christ of the Bible. It is a distorted image—a manufactured, painted on canvas, drawn from cheap theology Christ of the liberal, and the soft and timid person. This Christ has nothing of the iron and fury and anger, as well as the love and grace and mercy that He had, who walked in Galilee.

If I have a low concept of God, I will have a low concept of myself; and if I have a low conception of myself, I have a dangerous concept of sin. If I have a dangerous concept of sin, I have a degraded concept of Christ. Here is the way it works:

God is reduced; man is degraded; sin is underestimated; and Christ is disparaged.

Does this mean we must be tolerant? Actually, men are tolerant only with the unimportant things. What would happen to a tolerant scientist or a tolerant navigator? The liberal religionist simply admits that he does not consider spiritual things as vital.

No wonder Jude said the terrible things he said in his epistle to the Church. I recommend you read the book of Jude once. Get your teeth into something. Dare to believe something. And dare to stand for God. In this awful day of so-called tolerance, men are ready to believe anything.

We are not called to always show a smile. Sometimes we are called to frown and rebuke with all long-suffering and doctrine. We must contend but not be contentious. We must preserve truth but injure no man. We must destroy error without harming people. In earlier times, when men were wrong, they contended, and in contending, they became contentious. In an attempt to preserve truth, they destroyed those who held error. Let us preserve truth but injure no man.

Jude tells us, "These be they . . ." (Jude 1:19). Let us pity them, let us be sorry for them, let us pray for them and let us weep over them, but let us turn away from them. "But ye, beloved . . ." (v. 20). Now He's come to His own—true believers in God and in Christ. And then He gives them four things to do:

1. *Build up*—"building up yourselves on your most holy faith . . ." (v. 20). Do you have a Bible, and do you study it? Have you read a book of the Bible through recently? Have you done any memorization of Scripture? Have you sought to know God, or are you looking to the secular media for your religion? Build up yourselves on your most holy faith.

2. *Pray*—"praying in the Holy Ghost" (v. 20). I do not hesitate to say that most praying is not in the Holy Spirit. The reason is that we do not have the Holy Spirit in us. No man can pray in the Spirit except his heart is a habitation for the Spirit. It is only as the Holy Spirit has unlimited sway within you that you are able to pray in the Spirit. Five minutes of prayer in the Holy Spirit will be worth more than one year of hit-and-miss praying if it is not in the Holy Spirit.

3. *Love*—"keep yourselves in the love of God . . ." (v. 21). Be true to the faith, but be charitable to those who are in error. Never feel contempt for anybody. No Christian has any right to feel contempt, for it is an emotion that can only come out of pride. Let us never allow contempt to rule us; let us be charitable and loving toward all while we keep ourselves in the love of God.

4. *Look*—"looking for the mercy of our Lord Jesus Christ unto eternal life" (v. 21). Let us look for Jesus Christ's coming—for the mercy of the Lord Jesus Christ at His coming. Isn't it wonderful that His mercy will show forth at His coming? His mercy will show itself then, as it did on the cross; as it does in receiving sinners; as it does in patiently looking after us. And it will show itself at the coming of Jesus Christ unto eternal life.

Then Jude tells us, "Of some have compassion, making a difference: and others save with fear, pulling them out of the fire; hating even the garment spotted by the flesh" (v. 22). We are charged to win others; we should do everything in our power to win others to Christ, saving them with fear, pulling them out of the fire.

All his life, John Wesley referred to himself as "a brand plucked from the burning." He never called himself anything else. He knew that he was on fire with the hot flames of hell when Jesus Christ grabbed him out of the fiery pit and extinguished the fire by His own blood, and Wesley became Wesley. He never dared to rise and think of himself as a great Oxford man or a great genius; always he thought of himself as a brand plucked from the burning fire. We look forward to Jesus Christ's coming, looking for the mercy of our Lord Jesus Christ.

Here is what the old silk weaver, Gerhard Tersteegen (1697–1769), said about the Lord in his hymn "Oil and Wine" (see Isa. 35:10):

There is a balm for every pain,
    A medicine for all sorrow;
The eye turned backward to the Cross,
    And forward to the morrow.
The morrow of the glory and the psalm,
    When He shall come;
The morrow of the harping and the palm,
    The welcome home.
Meantime in His beloved hands our ways,
    And on His Heart the wandering heart at rest;
And comfort for the weary one who lays
    His head upon His Breast.

That is what Paul said: "Ye do shew the Lord's death till he come" (1 Cor. 11:26). Some of the old saints in days gone by called the Communion service the "medicine of immortality."

Meantime, what are we going to do? Give up to the evil? Give up to the liberals? Give up to the dead Church? Give up to those who have chosen to walk in the lowest shadow of Christian living?

Never.

Dare to contend without being contentious. Dare to preserve truth without hurting people. Dare to love and to be charitable.

Let us put our chin a little higher and our knees a little lower, and let us look a little further unto the throne of God for Jesus Christ, who sits at the right hand of God the Father Almighty. Let us be courageous but tender; severe but kind. And let us pray in the Holy Spirit and keep ourselves in the love of God, building up ourselves in the most holy faith, and win all those we can till the day of the glory and the song.

Faith of Our Fathers
Frederick William Faber (1814–1863)

Faith of our fathers, living still,
In spite of dungeon, fire and sword;
O how our hearts beat high with joy
Whenever we hear that glorious Word!

Faith of our fathers, we will strive
To win all nations unto Thee;
And through the truth that comes from God,
We all shall then be truly free.

Faith of our fathers, we will love
Both friend and foe in all our strife;

And preach Thee, too, as love knows how
By kindly words and virtuous life.

Faith of our fathers, holy faith!
We will be true to thee till death.

4

THE EFFECT OF SPIRITUAL LETHARGY

Awake, awake; put on thy strength, O Zion; put on thy beautiful garments, O Jerusalem, the holy city: for henceforth there shall no more come into thee the uncircumcised and the unclean. Shake thyself from the dust; arise, and sit down, O Jerusalem: loose thyself from the bands of thy neck, O captive daughter of Zion. For thus saith the LORD, Ye have sold yourselves for naught; and ye shall be redeemed without money.

ISAIAH 52:1-3

This familiar Old Testament passage in Isaiah describes a natural, national, literal revival yet to come. Although "Zion" refers to Israel, its spiritual content is for all who name the name of Israel's God in truth. I say this because sometimes men want to slough over what is written in the Old Testament as not applying to them; but Isaiah's words were fully applied to New Testament believers by John the Baptist, Christ Himself, Paul and other New Testament apostles and writers of epistles. They quoted Isaiah without hesitation and applied it directly, without excuse or apology, to the New Testament Church. If they did it, we can do it. And not only can we do it, but we should do it.

The Old Testament was for the Jews, but the spirit of the Old Testament is the same Spirit that wrote the New Testament. The same laws intrinsically apply; the same principles underlie the message. And while the dispensations change, the God of all dispensations has not changed.

This call "awake, awake" is addressed to sleeping people. To sleep is to be unconscious or semiconscious. It is to have a dimming of feeling and thought, and awareness is either absent or faint. When riding on a train, I sleep all night. In fact, I sleep better on a train than I do when I am not on a train; that is, I stay asleep longer. The lulling of the track must take me back to my childhood, because I am sort of nursed and rocked to sleep with the rhythmic beat of the wheels and the swaying of the train.

Yet I am never quite asleep, and the next day, I am rather groggy even though I slept all night. That is an odd situation, because while I am asleep, I am only partly asleep. There is an awareness that is not quite there and yet it is there, very faintly. The light never quite goes off; it just dims until you cannot read by it.

Some years ago, a man felt that he should take a walk one rainy night out to the little spur railroad. He did and found a man asleep across the rails, drunk. He picked him up, dragged him out of there before the coming freight train had ground him to bits. The rescued man was converted and became one of the church's songwriters and has lived a long and useful Christian life.

That man was asleep, in grave danger, and he didn't know it. He could have been killed there if somebody had not found him by a kind of divine providence. So it is with people who may be in a moral sleep. They may be in danger and not even know it. The danger may be approaching without giving the sleeper any concern at all.

This is why God says, "Awake, awake," and why Paul says, "Awake thou that sleepest . . . and Christ shall give thee light"

(Eph. 5:14). This kind of sleep leads to a condition of lethargy that has brought the evangelical Christian Church to a fearful state of spiritual bondage that manifests in contrasting areas—the moral and the spiritual.

A Moral Lethargy

Moral lethargy is to live and have habits and commit acts that are deeply rooted and hateful to God, without knowing it; these acts are dangerous to the soul. It is to live a life that is self-destructive and harmful to others and yet not be aware of it. It is to live a life that must certainly and surely lead directly to that place about which we do not like to speak, hell, and yet not be aware of it. This person is not alive, not worried, not concerned. He is in an absolute state of moral lethargy.

In the literature of the New England revivals, the word "awakening" was used. These revivals were called the "Great Awakening." People who had been morally asleep—careless men, women and young people—were suddenly awakened. I wonder if being "awakened" ought to be the word we use today.

"Can we be asleep and yet work?" Yes, we can be morally asleep and yet be intellectually awake. We can be morally asleep and yet run businesses, write, paint, work, travel, fly airplanes, play baseball, do anything men and women normally and properly might engage in. Not that what they are doing is wrong. Work is not wrong, but their lives are wrong.

It is entirely possible to be intellectually and physically awake and yet be morally asleep. I believe that is one thing wrong with us now; we sleep on in dangerous sin. Nobody likes to be awakened. Lying, cheating, gossiping and secret sinning, the miser and the grouch and the unbeliever—all of these may be deeply in sleep with the day of awakening not far away. I'm talking about the Day of Judgment; yet they sleep on.

Evangelists used to set out not to comfort people but to wake people up. They used to say, "You're asleep, and you'll be awakened by the trump of the archangel." That is too true of many people who are busy and happy, at peace and unconcerned, with their social enjoyments around them—their growing family, their comfortable homes. These are all proper and desirable and good things to have, but you can have them and still be morally asleep, not knowing how bad off you are.

A few sinners are semiconscious; they are slightly troubled but remain drowsy. A few others are deeply troubled but rather numb, like someone who is awake but not quite awake. I have been with people who were completely woozy for five or ten minutes after being asleep; you could not get through to them. I have met people who are deeply troubled, but numb. They are not awakened enough to do anything about it.

Some people, when they are converted, are converted the way I wake up after a night's sleep, with an absolute sudden awareness that has no drowsiness in it. Most people are not converted quite like that; they wake up a little more slowly. But it ought to be a complete awakening that rouses the sinner; that rouses the wrongdoer from his wrongdoings and the danger of them.

If you have been reared in a Christian home where the Bible, the Gospel, the Sunday School and the presence of Christian people have become a routine thing, and you're not affected by them at all; if even prayer does not affect you, that is a proof that you are morally asleep and need to wake up.

Spiritual Lethargy

Then there is another kind of sleep, and I do not know but what this might have been nearer to what the prophet Isaiah had in mind, and was certainly nearer to what Paul had in

54

mind when he said, "Awake thou that sleepest, and arise from the dead" (Eph. 5:14). Death is a spiritual sleep or lethargy. I would suppose that the moral man who was morally asleep was also spiritually asleep. It is possible for one to be morally awake and then slip back by degrees into a kind of spiritual somnolence that is coldness and lack of feeling about God and the things of God, about Christians and about the dying to self, and the Scriptures and prayer.

You get used to things and you get sophisticated. Spiritual sophistication lacks freshness and warmth; God is far away, and there is little communion and little joy in the Lord. To have a cold heart with little pity, little fire, little love and little worship is spiritual lethargy.

I believe that Christians ought to be careful that they are awake and stay awake; that they are alert to what is going on in the world. Most Christians are not alert to what is going on around them. They know it historically and in current events, but they do not know what the current events mean.

It is possible to have a television in every room and watch every news broadcast and subscribe to three papers and *TIME* magazine and *Newsweek* and still not know what is going on— not know the meaning of what is going on. I have noticed how religious journalism has gone to religious news items. Whole pages are devoted to religious news items. What this person did, what that person did and who was elected to this, who had a meeting over there, and who is the president of this college, and the arguments such-and-such had about baptism: news, everywhere, news.

It is possible to be crammed with religious news and filled with religious shoptalk and yet not have the spiritual discernment to know what it means. If there is anything I have asked God for, it is spiritual discernment. It makes you just about as popular as a hawk in a henhouse or a skunk at a picnic. You are not popular at all, and you will never be popular, because nobody wants to be awakened.

Somebody will say, "Mr. Tozer, I'm for you, in a general way, but I think you need correcting here on one thing: if somebody is asleep, how can you arouse him? The Bible says they are more than asleep, the Bible says the sinner's dead. How can you arouse dead men?" Some insist that it takes a convenient miracle of God's grace to sovereignly wake a man without his consent. After he has been sovereignly converted without his consent, he believes and is awake, and then you can preach to him.

Can a sleeping man be awakened? Can a person who is dead in sin be awakened? The technique and the psychology of it ought not to bother you; can you wake your 17-year-old son to go to high school? Can you? He is in deep sleep. At that age, they can go deep into sleep; they are nearly dead. Not a tense muscle anywhere. Deep sleep: how do you get him awake? Are you going to stand at his bedside and say to your husband, "George, according to my theology, this fellow is asleep and can't hear, therefore there's no use to try to wake him"? No church could ever have an awakening or a revival, and the prophet himself would be a fool for trying to awaken anybody.

Isaac Watts (1674–1748) wrote these terrible words:

Pursue the pleasures you design,
And cheer your hearts with songs and wine;
Enjoy the day of mirth, but know
There is a day of judgment, too.

But he went on to say this prayer:

Almighty God! Turn off their eyes
From these alluring vanities;
And let the thunder of Thy Word
Awake their souls to fear the Lord.

He knew it is possible to wake up the sleeper. It says, "Shake thyself from the dust and put on the beautiful garments" and in the Bible, garments, of course, are righteousness and true holiness; basic goodness, moral soundness. I was taught for a long time that "There is none righteous, no, not one," and therefore to say someone is a "good man" is to insult God. The Bible says, "For he was a good man, and full of the Holy Ghost and of faith: and much people was added unto the Lord" (Acts 11:24).

A Christian ought to be, above all other things, a good man. If he is not basically a good man, I cannot see how he can be a Christian. Now, he is not good by nature. By nature, he is, as theologian and author Loraine Boettner (1901–1990) said, "An alien by birth and a sinner by choice." Everybody who has been truly converted knows that. When God converts a man, he not only writes the man's name in the Lamb's book of life and justifies him from his past sins, but He also makes him to become a good man.

A man wrote me and said, "I have been reading Finney. I am simply astonished to learn that Charles G. Finney expected as much of a converted man as we now expect of a man after he has been filled with the Holy Spirit. Finney would not grant a man to even be converted unless he showed a purity of life that we now call sanctification; he started where we end." That was Finney, which was why 75 percent of his converts stood. Finney insisted that basically a man ought to put on his beautiful garments if he is going to serve the Lord Jesus, and not use the Lord Jesus simply as a means of getting something.

Sydney J. Harris (1917–1986), a columnist for the *Chicago Daily News*, was a theatrical critic as well as a general philosopher. In one of his columns, he wrote a little paragraph in which he said, "The modern religious revival leaves me cold for this reason. Men are trying to use God in place of offering themselves to God to be used by Him." He then added these words: "No man has a right to ask God for peace of mind unless it's founded on righteousness." The children of this world are wiser in their generation than the children of the day. Every once in a while, in some liberal university somewhere, or out in some place where you would not expect any light at all to come, somebody will make a pronouncement that is like a flash of lightning in the darkness, telling us that if we do not look out, we will be using God to get peace of mind, to get business, to get rich, and never serve God at all.

If God never answered another prayer for me as long as I live, I still want God to know that I want to serve Him until I die. If He never did another thing for me from this day on, if He withdrew His hand and let me go to pieces physically, mentally, emotionally, financially and every other way, I would still want Him to know I want to serve Him just because He is God.

The modern emphasis that God is a convenience and Jesus Christ so kindly died for us in order that we might have peace of mind is a travesty of the gospel. Sinners know it, and the liberals know it. Only we poor, lethargic evangelicals fail to see it.

Basic goodness, moral soundness and purity of life, honesty that will not cheat tax collectors or anybody else, truthfulness that will not lie about any person more than is present, mercy, humbleness, and forgiving love. What a sight that is, to put on the beautiful garments, and there are some. Thank

God, there are some people here and there throughout the world who wear the beautiful garments of righteousness and true holiness, and walk with their God. They are not popular and not heard of much, but they quietly walk with their God.

Thomas Gray (1716–1771), in his masterpiece "Elegy Written in a Country Churchyard," said that many a mute Milton had walked here, among these hedgerows and through the shocks of corn, filled with everything that Milton knew but was unable to express:

> Some village-Hampden, that with dauntless breast
> The little tyrant of his fields withstood,
> Some mute inglorious Milton here may rest,
> Some Cromwell, guiltless of his country's blood.

I believe there are mute, inglorious Pauls and Davids walking the earth today. These are simple, plain, godly people who believe in the power of the blood of Jesus not only to save us from hell but also to cleanse us now on earth.

They are not heard of maybe, they are "mute inglorious Miltons," but they are among us. They are the seeds, yet, of survival. "Put on thy strength," it says, and in the Bible, of course, that means the power of the Holy Spirit. "Awake, awake; put on thy strength, O Zion; put on thy beautiful garments, O Jerusalem, the holy city: for henceforth there shall no more come into thee the uncircumcised and the unclean" (Isa. 52:1).

Unless there is an awakening out of our spiritual lethargy, this generation of Christians is being set up to backslide as no other generation before. I pray that all of us who are awake now will do our duty and our privilege, and our right under grace, to be filled with the Holy Spirit so that we might rise, shine and let our light shine forth to the world. It is time we wake up.

Ye Sons of Adam, Vain and Young
Isaac Watts (1674–1748)

Ye sons of Adam, vain and young,
Indulge your eyes, indulge your tongue,
Taste the delights your souls desire,
And give a loose to all your fire;

Pursue the pleasures you design,
And cheer your hearts with songs and wine;
Enjoy the day of mirth, but know
There is a day of judgment, too.

God from on high records your thoughts,
His book records your secret faults;
The works of darkness you have done
Must all appear before the sun.

The vengeance to your follies due
Should strike your hearts with terror through:
How will you stand before His face,
Or answer for His injured grace?

Almighty God! Turn off their eyes
From these alluring vanities;
And let the thunder of Thy Word
Awake their souls to fear the Lord.

5

THE PROCESS OF BACKSLIDING

The backslider in heart shall be filled with his own ways: and a good man shall be satisfied from himself.

PROVERBS 14:14

The backsliding Christian is one of the most serious threats to plague the evangelical church today. If the Church is to complete the job of world evangelization before the return of Christ, we need to deal with this serious problem.

The word "backsliding" came from the backward slide of Israel, reminiscent of a backsliding heifer. I have seen that happen as a lad on the farm, when an animal would start up a slippery bank, get partway up and then lose traction and slip back after many plunges and efforts to get up. Sometimes it could not get up at all. The man of God, with no intention of being facetious, said that Israel was like the animals he had seen try to climb up a slippery hill. They worked hard at it and pushed, and then they slid back as many steps as they had gone up.

The Fickle Heart

There are two main causes of backsliding. The first cause is *the fickleness of the human heart*. It would be a wonderful thing if we could remain what we were, but it would also be a most damning thing. How sad our state would be if we could not change. Our ability to change our mind is our hope.

The call of God in repentance is a call to change from the worst state to a better state. If we could not go from one state to another, we would be morally static; we would be damned. Because it is possible to go from one moral state to another, we can go from bad to good and can get right with God. We can become good, though we were bad before; we can become holy, though we were unholy before. That same ability to go from one moral state to another and to change our mind can also cause us not to backslide.

The caution is that the only thing people stick to, as a rule, is something that nature forces them to do—eating, drinking, sleeping, self-protection or some other strong internal instinct. As long as the human race goes on, there will always be love, marriage and all that, because it is a deeply rooted instinct in human nature. But anything that requires planning and careful, painstaking labor is easy to turn away from.

People tend to follow what is easy and what goes the natural way. Outside of taxes and certain other duties forced upon us from the outside, either by nature or by law, we mostly do what we like to do or what is natural to us. That is fertile soil for backsliding. A person under some great pressure of bereavement or fear turns to God for a while, but the instinct to stay there is not in them. The instinct is to go the other way. It is irksome, this reading the Bible and praying. It turns into a painstaking thing, and so it eats away a little at a time until a person has gone backward.

If you took a poll of every man and woman who, under evangelistic pressure, made some step toward God, you would see that today they have forgotten all about Him. They are now living as if there were no God in heaven above. I tell you, it would be a shock you would not get over if you could see them all in some stadium, standing like statues, tier on tier. Though some made a step toward God, or even met God, it did not last, because serving Jesus Christ is contrary to the human nature. By nature, we do not persevere. The fickleness of the human heart turns a person away, and he backslides.

The Evil Heart

Then there is the *inherent evil of the human heart* that causes backsliding. The whole constitution of a human being is against being good. Remember two things here. If we are now what we originally were, made in the image of God, without sin, then it would be perfectly natural to serve God as the angels in heaven above and the seraphim beside the throne have no trouble serving God. Nothing in them pulls them away from God.

When made to serve God, a being is doing what is as natural to its nature as a duck when it goes to the water. A duck is following its nature; and the holy angels above follow their nature to serve God. If you and I were what we should be, unfallen and without the taint and stain of sin, we would be able to serve God as the angels do, and it would come natural and flow out like a fountain from the pressure beneath. But we are fallen.

A man turns his face to do that which anciently he did in Adam and should be doing now; but sin has robbed him of the power. Sin made our nature. So when we pray, it is not natural. All of us have to accumulate the wages of sin, if we say, "Our Father, who art in Heaven." But if that sin had not come to override, we would simply raise our voices and, like the bird, we would sing God's praises without moving away from Him and cooling off.

Backsliding always begins with the heart. People blame other circumstances and say, "It's my home life. It's the place where I work. It's the school. It's because I was ill, or it was because I had to work too much. It's because I didn't have time." Those are external things; backsliding begins in the heart.

God knows before an individual knows when his heart is cooling off. After God, the individual finds it out. Then the church finds it out; and if he continues, the world finds it out. This is always the order. At the point when the world finds out a man or woman has backslidden and gone back on his faith, the church knew it before the world, and the individual knew it before the church; but God knew it before the man or woman found it out. Backsliding always begins in the human heart.

What Happens in the Backsliding Heart

What is happening in the person with a backsliding heart? To begin with, he is losing interest in the things of God and gradually going back to the old ways or to more refined sins than the ones he used to do. He is losing interest toward God. His heart is not as hot as it was a few weeks or months or a year before, and his love toward God is cooling off.

Then, he is losing interest in communion with God. If you are not doing as well as you used to, the only kind and honest thing I can say is that you are a backslider in heart. If you loved to pray before, you will love to pray as much now. If you do not love to pray as much as before, at what other conclusion can you arrive?

If the doctor takes a blood count and finds the blood count way down, what can he do? Or if he runs other tests and finds that the man's health is in trouble, what honest thing can a doctor do? He's not going to pat him on the shoulder and say, "I'll meet you on the golf course Saturday. Everything will be all right." What a fool that doctor would be, and what a traitor to his profession. There is only one thing for him to do. He must state his findings and say, "Bud, you're not in as good a shape as you used to be. You ought to listen to me now." And then the doctor gives his patient suggestions for improving his health.

The point is that the honest doctor will tell a patient if he runs tests and finds there is a problem with his health.

Backsliding is the losing of our individual communion with God. Read an old hymnbook and see how the writers loved to fellowship with God. Communion with God was sweet to them. We have so much these days that crowds our time for communion with God—so many things that distract us from being quiet before Him.

Backsliding resides in the heart, and these other things are only external aids to the devil. When a man is backslidden in heart, he tends to get a little bit bored. If a glowing, earnest Christian bores you a little; if when you are in a little group drinking coffee or soda, and it bores you a little or embarrasses you when somebody brings up the thought of God, you had better look to your own heart. Whenever talk of God and His Word and His work in the world bores us, be sure that we are wrong inside.

To be as honest and realistic as possible, I will say that some people are religious bores. They have a way of introducing religion into the most impossible situations and do it out of habit, without sincerity or any spontaneity whatsoever, but only because they have been trained to do it, like trained seals. They would bore an archangel. But if an honest, happy-hearted Christian turns and talks about God, and it bores you or embarrasses you, you are in the wrong company. If you are bored with spiritual conversation (I'm not talking about religious chitchat that would bore anybody), something has gone wrong inside of your heart. The best thing to do is admit it and acknowledge it before God.

Another symptom is the presence of a critical spirit toward other preachers. If he is not a Billy Graham, some people do not want to hear him. When a plain, good, honest man gets up, and with poor delivery and a few blunders tells them about God and the things of God, they will say, "Oh, he's all right." They will come in small numbers but with no zeal or enthusiasm unless it is an extraordinary preacher. I tell you, we could well afford to humble ourselves and listen to anyone that has something to say. I think we ought to pray, "God, give me a heart so sensitive that I'll get help from anyone." I'm not talking about getting help from hypocrites and pretenders; nobody can get help from them. I do not look to the devil for my help, but to any honest man of God.

We ought to be careful lest we become too professional and develop the tendency to criticize unkindly. If it is a question of trying to improve, that is another matter. If it is a question of trying to push the standards up—to get people to write, preach, pray, talk and exhort better, to help the new choir to raise its standards—that is another matter and is perfectly all right. But if it is just carping, I do not care to hear him. If the man writes or sings, and he is a sincere man, then he ought to warm my heart with his sincerity if I am not backslidden.

If all the people entering churches on a given Sunday are cooling off in their hearts or have cooled off and do not have in their hearts what their presence seems to show they have, many a pastor would spend the afternoon on his face, weeping between the porch and the altar, crying, "Oh, what have I done or haven't done, that my people are in such a condition?"

Solomon wrote, "The backslider in heart shall be filled with his own ways: and a good man shall be satisfied from himself" (Prov. 14:14). It means the backslider will soon get enough of himself. How? He gets enough of himself when he attempts to pray and finds how heavy and embarrassed he is to be devout. He is asked to pray and he tries to be devout, but his heart has long ago broken fellowship. He is like an instrument ready to be plugged in where there is no power. He plugs in dutifully, but nothing happens. A man gets enough of that after a while, and enough of hollow testimonies. They are false and the words are dry. Yet he dare not stop talking, because he's got a reputation for being a good Christian.

Many people have a reputation for being good Christians in churches; then they secretly break with God and there is a lack of communion. The fires burn low and they hardly feel any sense of God at all; and yet they have to keep it up, so they may even allow themselves to get elected to boards and to young people's groups, to choirs and all the rest. I am afraid the whole thing is hopeless, because the heart has slipped away. When God finds our hearts slipping, and we will not admit it to ourselves in our secret moments, we have gotten to a place where, if we told the truth, we are bored with God and religion. We would not admit it—we would be ashamed to admit it—but there it is.

What do you think God thinks about us? Jesus, in the book of Revelation, said, "Nevertheless I have somewhat against thee, because thou hast left thy first love" (2:4). He chided that church because He found it happening back in the second century. He chided them because they were losing their affection but would not admit it. Not an elder in the Ephesian church who stood to preach; not a deacon that ever passed the plates; not a member of the board would ever dare to get up and say, "I'm tired of God. I'm weary of this whole business." Jesus said, "I don't feel the warmth I used to feel. Your smile is not there; your breath is not so warm; the tone of your voice is not so affectionate. I miss it," He said. "You've left your first love." After a while, a man will get enough of that—of trying to keep up religious appearances with a hollow testimony and talk with enthusiastic Christians about God, and seeming to enjoy it.

Some are bored with constant church attendance. Some-body has told them: Don't send your children to Sunday School; get out of bed and take them. They determine they are going to follow that admonition, and it is good. I am glad they do, but it would be so much better if they enjoyed it. I have been forced to go to religious meetings that I did not want to attend. I knew there was nothing there for me; I could not con-tribute anything, but I had gone because circumstances com-pelled me. If I have to be doing something I do not like to do, I would get bored with that right early. That is evidence of something I do not like to think about.

Then, there is the matter of giving; God's warm-hearted people give spontaneously. They love it. They give joyously, be-cause it is a pleasure to give.

If I were not a Christian, I would not tithe. All of those button pushers that come along and try to show that if you tithe you'll have more money than you did if you don't tithe; all of that low-grade effort to get people to give isn't Chris-tian; it isn't spiritual; it isn't decent. What kind of person would you be if you brought your offerings to God's house knowing that if you did you would be more prosperous than if you did not? Knowing that you will have more than if you did not tithe? That's tithing to get more. What kind of person would you be?

When you have lost your joy, you will get tired of giving out of habit. The man will get enough of that after a while, and I pray the sooner the better, and keep cheerful. Keep spir-itually cheerful and relax. In Galatians 6:1, Paul tells us, "Brethren, if a man be overtaken in a fault, ye which are spir-itual, restore such a one." The words used there are medical terms and mean that when an arm or shoulder gets out of joint, it gets snapped back in. I pray that God will do us the inestimable favor of going from heart to heart, mind to mind and soul to soul—that He will test us with His spiritual Geiger counter. And if there is a cooling off in there, He will find it and cure it.

Remember when Jesus looked upon Peter. Scripture says, "And the Lord turned, and looked upon Peter. And Peter remembered the word of the Lord, how he had said unto him, Before the cock crow, thou shalt deny me thrice. And Peter went out, and wept bitterly" (Luke 22:61-62).

I do not know what Jesus said. He simply turned and looked at Peter. The woman said, "Are you one of His followers?" and Peter said, "No."

She said, "It's your accent."

He said, "I'm not."

She said again, "You are. Your speech betrays you."

Then he said, "I'm not a Christian. I am going to do something no Christian would do." So he cursed. His actions were saying that if he acted like a Christian, he might be arrested along with Jesus. So in order to prove that he was not a Christian, he was going to curse, and so he cursed.

She finally said, "Oh, well he's right. He is not a Christian."

Just before He died, Jesus turned and looked at that cursing apostle. Peter was not well educated, but he was a genius in his own right, and he looked up into that face, and what he saw in that face of hurt and pain and sorrow and longing and love was too much for Peter. He hurried out of the house and stood outside somewhere, and with his face in his hands, he wept bitterly. The Greek language indicates an uncontrolled torrent of weeping; yet Jesus never said a word. He just looked at Peter.

I wonder if the tender Jesus will not look at you—just look, that is all. How will you respond?

What Will You Do with Jesus?
A. B. Simpson (1843–1919)

Jesus is standing in Pilate's hall,
Friendless, forsaken, betrayed by all;
Hearken! what meaneth the sudden call?
What will you do with Jesus?

Jesus is standing on trial still,
You can be false to Him if you will,
You can be faithful through good or ill:
What will you do with Jesus?

Will you evade him as Pilate tried?
Or will you choose Him, whate'er betide?
Vainly you struggle from Him to hide:
What will you do with Jesus?

Will you, like Peter, your Lord deny?
Or will you scorn from His foes to fly,
Daring for Jesus to live or die?
What will you do with Jesus?

"Jesus, I give Thee my heart today!
Jesus, I'll follow Thee all the way,
Gladly obeying Thee!" will you say:
"This I will do with Jesus!"

What will you do with Jesus?
Neutral you cannot be;
Some day your heart will be asking,
"What will He do with me?"

6

THE IRREPRESSIBLE LAW OF CONSEQUENCE

Thus saith the LORD of hosts; consider your ways.

HAGGAI 1:7

The human mind is so constituted that it must consider something; so it compromises by considering other people's ways. The Pharisees were a class of people who knew the sins of everybody but themselves. They considered the sins of the harlot, the tax collector and the drunkard, but they never considered their own sin at all. A voice is speaking to us in the Word and out of heaven, saying, "Consider your ways"—look closely and consider seriously.

All society conspires to prevent us from doing this. Organized human society wants us to do everything but consider our ways. Yet this is more important than any or all the objects demanding your attention. You may give consideration to a house, a car, travel or health—to any one of a number of legitimate things. Yet more important than any branch of learning you might engage in anywhere, at any time, you are to give careful, serious, intelligent and honest consideration to your ways. When the Scripture says, "Consider your ways," it means consider your moral ways. Notice that it is your own ways you are to consider, which is contrary to our common habit. And it is the work of the Holy Spirit to focus our attention there.

The Law of Consequence

Everything is related to its past and its future. Every act committed, everything that exists, every word you utter and every deed you do is related to the past as a consequence and to the future as an effect, which produces another consequence. The simple illustration is that of the egg in the nest. The egg lying in the nest is an effect of another act, the previous act of the bird that laid it. While it is a consequence of an act, it is also the cause of another thing, and that is the new bird that will be hatched. It is a link between what was and what will be. Just so is every thought you have and every deed you do a link between something that made you do or think or say this thing and that which will be the result of your having said or thought or done this thing.

Everything has a consequence. The curse and the blessing do not come causeless. Everything is an effect of something else. Not only is everything a consequence of something else, but it also has consequences in something else. The simplest word you have uttered today was a result of some conditioning of your mind and heart yesterday. And your words will have consequences tomorrow. They may only be mild, but there will be consequences. Everything you are, say, do or think is a result of some choice you made in the past and will result in some future saying, doing, being or thinking.

Everything has consequences of dual importance. It is important for what it is in itself and it is important for what it causes to be. Being intelligent and moral creatures, we are accountable for our acts. I think it would make a wonderful difference in our lives if we were to remember, and believe, that we are going to give an account to God for every deed and every word.

I am not sure, but this may be, finally and at last, the most vitally important thing about consequences and acts and effects and causes; that is, what everything does to our own moral structure—what it does to our lives. For what we are will determine our destiny. Our moral fabric will determine heaven or hell for us.

The act of accepting Christ, if it is a true act, has an instant effect upon our entire moral life, and it changes the man from being a bad man to being a good man. God will not, by some trick of grace, take evil, foul-minded, self-righteous and vile people into his heaven. When He saves a man, He saves him from sin. If he is not saved from sin, he is not saved at all! There is no act of grace and no trick of mercy and no justification that can take an unholy man into the presence of God or an evil man into God's holy heaven. He came not to call the righteous but sinners to repentance. He came not to call people who thought they were righteous but people who knew they were sinful. When He calls us to Himself and saves us, He saves us out of our past and out of our iniquity; and by a threefold act of justification, regeneration and sanctification, He makes people fit for heaven.

It's an erroneous idea that justification is an imparted robe of righteousness put over a dirty, filthy fellow who terribly needs a bath and is filled with cooties and the accumulation of the dirt of a lifetime, who stands boldly in God Almighty's holy heaven, among seraphim and cherubim and archangels and the spirits of just men made perfect, and blithely and flippantly says, "I belong in hell. I'm a filthy man but what are you going to do about it? I have on me the robe of Christ's righteousness and that's enough."

God saves only sinners, and He saves only sinners who know they are sinners. He saves only sinners who admit they are sinners; but He saves sinners and turns them from being sinners to being good men and full of the Holy Spirit. When we teach anything else, we are teaching heresy. John Newton was a Puritan and would have been horrified if he had heard the doctrines we are hearing now.

I say that each act has consequences in our moral structure, in what we are, which is the most important thing about you. Nobody fools me by his dress. And certainly nobody fools the Holy Spirit. Nobody impresses the Holy Spirit by how good-looking he is or by the color of his skin. Nobody impresses the Holy Spirit with his education or degrees or where he has been. Our choices have consequences in our moral structure, either to strengthen virtue or to rot the nerve center of virtue. You have met people whose virtue has been rotted at the core, like a tree ready to crash to the ground.

Then it also has a secondary consequence in what it does to others. No man lives unto himself. Either directly or indirectly, you are deeply influencing somebody else. If you are a carelessly living Christian, there may be persons who will use your careless life as a shield, a hiding place for his own much more serious iniquity. Or there may be those who kneel at night and say, "God, make me like brother So-and-so, make me like Mrs. So-and-so." It can be both ways, for deeds have consequences and are the result of choices, whether they are impulsive choices or carefully thought out choices.

The Vital Act of Choice

No act has as far-reaching a consequence as the act of choosing. Everything we are is a result of choices we have made. What we are today is a result of choices we made yesterday; everything we will be tomorrow will be the result of choices we make today. Those choices may be good or bad; they may be ignorant or well advised; they may be impulsive or made after much thought; they may be made out of spite.

A young couple has a fight, and the girl rushes out, marries somebody else and says, "I'll show that twerp!" Then she lives with her second choice for a lifetime and whispers to people, "This was the mistake of my life!" Selfish choices, cowardly choices, choices made because we are afraid to make other ones. We can make our choices wise, unselfish, far-seeing, courageous, humble, faith-inspired, God-obeying choices.

A person's choices distinguish him as either wise or foolish. The wise man knows he must give account of the deeds done in the body, but the fool does not. In the Bible, the word "fool" is not describing a man of mental deficiency. A fool is a man who acts without regard to consequences.

However, it is deeper than morals, for morals have to do with ethics, righteousness and our relationship to our fellow man and to self. It is in the spirit of the man. In the Bible, a wise man is not necessarily an educated man or one of high cultural level, although he could be. A wise man is a man who acts with an eye to consequences. He thinks, "What will the result of this be?" Then he acts in a way that will bring him consequences he will not have to be ashamed of or afraid of in the day to come. This explains the difference between wisdom and folly as God sees it.

An educated man, a man of some standing in the neighborhood, a wealthy man, a man who looked ahead but a man who never thought beyond his last heartbeat. He was a fool. Our Lord said so. Hell is full of fools and heaven is full of wise men. There will never be a fool in heaven, and there will never be a wise man in hell. According to God's definition, a fool is one who acts without regard to consequences and who chooses without thinking of eternity. Nobody like that will be in heaven. Heaven will be filled with the opposite.

The idea that God loves evil men and cannot stand a decent man is a modern heresy. It is not true and never was true. There is nothing in the Bible to lead us to believe that it is true. But if the evil man became wise long enough to make his eternal choice in the light of eternal consequences, and he chose God and Christ and the blood of the Lamb and repentance and deliverance from sin, he is a wise man, and God accounts him such; and heaven will be filled with such.

Fools chose whom they wanted to marry, but they did not think of eternity when they did it. They chose what they wanted to do with their money, and they did it. They chose what they were going to say, and they thought, *Our mouths are our own; our tongues belong to us. Who can tell us what to say with our tongues?* Therefore, they said what they would, but they did not think of tomorrow, of the judgment day, of the awful face of God or the Great White Throne. They were fools.

Hell is full of fools, and heaven is full of wise men. There are wise men in heaven that could not read and write when they were on earth; and there are learned fools in hell that had degrees after their name like the tail on a kite. They knew everything but the one thing: They were fools.

Choose Well Today

Our main choice is choosing between life and death. What we shall choose has been left to our own decision. "Choose you this day," says the Holy Spirit. What we choose is left to us. If a man cannot sin, he cannot be holy. If he cannot sin, he is not free; and if he is not free, he cannot be holy. Free choice is as necessary to holiness as it is to sin. Holiness is moral freedom of choice resulting in a right choice of holiness and righteousness. Nobody ever deliberately chooses death. As Tennyson said:

No matter what crazy sorrow saith
No man that ever breathed with mortal breath
Has ever really longed for death.
'Tis life, not death, for which we pant.

Nobody ever longs for death; they simply choose the path that leads there. They have chosen it by a series of small choices. They have made the last choice of moral folly. They have chosen death; not that they looked at death and said, "I choose you!" but they looked at all the pleasant ways that lead there and said, "I choose you."

Cities do not choose to rot and die; they just choose to do that which leads them to rot and die. And just as men do not choose life or death, they do not choose life in itself. No man can stand up and say, "I choose life" in that sense. He says, "I choose the one who gives life; I choose the way to life. I choose life by repudiating death."

The Bible says "Choose you this day, choose life." However, you have to come where the life is. You choose water, but you come where the water is and you drink. You choose to be saved, but you have to come where the Lord and Savior is to be saved and give yourself into His hands. We make the right choice by starting with repentance.

There are people that would influence you. Some would be better Christians if they were not under the influence of those who are not good Christians. Some are being influenced to make wrong choices. Those who influence you are blind, hard, calloused or morally irresponsible, and they cannot help you in that last day.

The fellow who is leading you off, who is influencing you now and leading you away, will say in that day, "What's that to me? I cannot answer for you. See you to that!" That business partner who is persuading you to cut edges, cut corners and be a bit crooked, smiles, pats your back and tells people, "Good old Joe, he's a great guy, ha-ha." However, there will be a day when "good old Joe" will stand all by himself—that will be you—and your business partner will not be able to help you at all.

I want to influence you, if you are living a casual Christian life, to consider your ways and start living a Christian life that will shame the devil and please God and start you on the way to victorious living and fruitful service and holy character.

You must make the choice. That choice will result in deeds, and those deeds will result in destiny. God has bestowed this honor upon you that you can choose. Have you chosen the one who gives life?

Grace and Consequences Coexist

One of the characteristics of spiritual lethargy is misunderstanding the law of consequence. For some reason, many Christians have the idea that when they are born again, they do not have to deal with consequences. Therefore, many live a life of flagrant disregard for the idea of consequence. After all, so they say, "I'm living by grace."

Nobody would ever question the fact that King David was a godly man. The Bible even says of him that he was a man after God's own heart (see Acts 13:22). Yet this godly man suffered immensely in this area of consequence. With all of the victories this man had, it would be easy to assume that he did not have to worry about this.

The story of David and Bathsheba is well known to all who read the Scriptures (see 2 Sam. 11–12). It was one of the darkest moments in David's life. He made certain choices, and because of those choices, certain consequences materialized. For every deed there is a corresponding consequence.

For David, the deed was his adulterous relationship with Bathsheba. This deed was a choice that he alone made and bore the responsibility for. The consequence was the death of his and Bathsheba's child. No matter how much David pleaded with God to spare the life of this child, the child died. A scriptural principle that is often misconstrued is found in Galatians 6:7: "Be not deceived; God is not mocked: for whatsoever a man soweth, that shall he also reap." This is the irrepressible law of consequence.

Because of the growing spiritual apathy among many Christians, we often make choices without any consideration whatsoever for the consequences that follow. Or, we have cultivated the spirit of misdirected expectation. By that, I mean our expectation is not associated with our choices. Make no mistake: Today you face the consequences of yesterday's choices. Tomorrow you will face the consequences of today's choices.

Victory Through Grace
Fanny J. Crosby (1820–1915)

Conquering now and still to conquer,
rideth a King in His might;
Leading the host of all the faithful
into the midst of the fight;
See them with courage advancing,
clad in their brilliant array,
Shouting the Name of their Leader,
hear them exultingly say:

Not to the strong is the battle,
not to the swift is the race,
Yet to the true and the faithful vict'ry
is promised through grace.

Conquering now and still to conquer,
who is this wonderful King?
Whence are the armies which He leadeth,
while of His glory they sing?
He is our Lord and Redeemer,
Savior and Monarch divine;
They are the stars that forever bright
in His kingdom shall shine.

Conquering now and still to conquer,
Jesus, Thou Ruler of all,
Thrones and their scepters all shall perish,
crowns and their splendor shall fall,
Yet shall the armies Thou leadest,
faithful and true to the last,
Find in Thy mansions eternal rest,
when their warfare is past.

PART II

· · · · · · · · · · · · ·

THE CHALLENGES FACING THE EVANGELICAL CHURCH

7

THE SOURCES OF DANGER IN THE CHURCH

I will love thee, O LORD, my strength. The LORD is my rock, and my
fortress, and my deliverer; my God, my strength, in whom I will trust;
my buckler, and the horn of my salvation, and my high tower.

PSALM 18:1-2

Spiritual lethargy has brought the evangelical church to the brink of apostasy and put the average Christian in an extremely vulnerable and challenging position. It is virtually impossible to help a person until he comes to the point of realizing he needs help and in what areas of life he needs help. So, the first step is to know what the dangers are, followed decisively by knowing how to deal with the dangers at hand.

First, we need spiritual discernment. We need Christians whose eyes have been opened to see the treacherous condition the Church faces today and to show the way out. Along with discernment, we need courage to speak out against those dangers and call the Church back to her Rock, Jesus Christ.

In his day, David understood the seriousness of the dangers in the way. The dangers he faced are essentially the same dangers we are facing today; and the way David dealt with those dangers is the same way we must deal with them today. The psalms of David are a reflective image of the Christian life. All of life's experiences are found in the psalms—life's dangers, joys, sadness, victories, work, labor and defeat. You will find life's night and life's day, her shadows and her sunshine—even life and death itself.

The book of Psalms is a mirror of spiritual life. In Psalm 18, we find words that indicate obvious dangers in the Christian way—dangers from which we must escape or know how to meet and conquer. Since real dangers to the spiritual life do exist, it is proper that God's people should be alerted to them. Any shepherd desiring to be a faithful shepherd should point them out to the people and also point a way of escape. It is no good to examine the patient if you do not have a cure. It is no good to warn of the danger of attack if you do not have a bomb shelter. It is no good to know that your enemy is coming if you do not know how to meet your enemy.

Danger approaches the Christian life from three directions: *the world* through which we journey, *the god of this world* and *our unmortified flesh*. That's why we need a rock, a fortress, a deliverer, a buckler, a high tower to run to—all names for God.

The World

When I say that the world is a source of danger to the Christian, I do not mean the wind, the storm, the lightning, the sea and the desert, all of which are beautiful and wonderful. These are not the dangers we need to be concerned about. I know there is danger from the lightning, but it is not the real danger David is thinking of in Psalm 18.

In Psalm 18, David was not concerned about the dangers of the natural world. He was thinking as a spiritual man, and he might have been thinking of his physical enemies; but always

David saw the spiritual side of things. The Holy Spirit did not put this psalm in His Word to remind us that there is danger from nature. You can destroy a human body and not injure the spirit of the man at all. You can tear down the temple and not hurt the spirit that dwells within. You can cause a man's bones to lie in the desert, but the man's spirit can be unharmed in the presence of His Father and God. Real dangers are dangers that get through to the soul and the spirit of a man.

The soldiers cut off John the Baptist's head but did not hurt John at all. When our Savior died on the cross, His body was destroyed, it was broken for us; but the man, Christ Jesus, was preserved in the bosom of God. So was Paul when they cut off his head. The apostle said, "Henceforth there is laid up for me a crown of righteousness, which the Lord, the righteous judge, shall give me at that day: and not to me only, but unto all them also that love his appearing" (2 Tim. 4:8). Paul went to that crown, rather than to defeat, when they executed him. No real harm can come through the physical body to a man, only through the soul.

What then do we mean by the world when we say that real dangers come to the Christian through the world? The threat comes to us through human society outside the will of God. As long as sin remains, human society will be a threat to the Christian soul. Human society's sin, unbelief, diversions, ambitions, however skillfully disguised, are a threat to the Christian soul.

That is why the Bible is so stern and insistent about the world. Many Christian leaders will apologize and compromise and smooth things over with the world. But you will find nothing but stern insistence in the Bible that we ought to forsake the world and not in any way be influenced by its sin or unbelief or diversions or ambitions or worldly spirit. The dangers that come to the Christian come through this world.

Many have been living off the world, riding on the carcass of the world, and then when it goes into the gutter, gracefully pulling away just in time. "How far can I go and still not go over? Tell me what I can do and still not be lost? Just how far can I go?" One of these days the person who does this is going to get caught in the world with no viable exit strategy.

The God of This World

The devil is called by four names in the Bible: dragon, serpent, the devil and Satan. He is called the dragon in such places as Revelation 12, when he is in government. When the devil in the Roman Empire was busy destroying the Church, they said, "He's like the dragon."

Approximately 13,000,000 Christians perished around the city of Rome in the first two centuries. As they saw their loved ones led away and beheaded, one after the other, I can see how they said, "This is the dragon; this is the devil in government." Based on the 6,000,000 Jews that died under Hitler, in gas chambers and by other means and methods of execution, I can see how they might say, "Satan is in this man, Hitler, and he's thrashing his dirty, destructive tail around and killing people."

Whenever the devil gets into government and starts persecuting, the Bible calls him the dragon. I do not say the devil is in every government. I am not saying that politicians are devil-possessed men. I am only saying there are times when this dragon can so wind himself into government that he takes it over and starts his destructiveness. He is the dragon when he is destroying.

Another name for him is the serpent. Same person, only he has a different mask on this time, and he would not hurt you for the world. He would not kill you; he would not put you in jail; he would not cut off your head. He is wily, smiling and slick-tempered; works by cunning and deception and wins by compromise, tolerance and patience. He gets your confidence and then sells you the Brooklyn Bridge. This smooth, slick serpent is the "confidence man of hell," with his tricks and his cunning and his deceitfulness.

Satan did not go to the desert to destroy Jesus with a blow on the head. He went and said, "Speak to these stones that they be made bread." He knew that if Jesus, the Son of God, had listened and spoken to a stone and done a miracle outside of the will of God, he would have destroyed the Savior of the world more easily than if he had a put a spear through His heart. However, Satan did not tell Jesus that. It was a compromise. He said, "Poor you, you're hungry, aren't you?" Patted His shoulder and whispered, "Poor you, why don't you get some bread? You've got the power, you know you have."

Jesus said, "It is written, Man shall not live by bread alone, but by every word that proceedeth out of the mouth of God" (Matt. 4:4).

Satan said, "I'll give you all the kingdoms of the world."

Jesus said, "Get thee hence, Satan: for it is written, Thou shalt worship the Lord thy God, and him only shalt thou serve" (Matt. 4:10). It was all so slick. The devil is a smooth salesman—the wrong kind. He will sell you anything.

My intention is not to make you devil conscious, even though I am talking about the god of this world. I have met Christians who are jumpy because of the devil. The best thing to do is to keep your eyes on Jesus and let Him take care of the devil.

In boxing, there is such a thing as a puncher and a counterpuncher. A counterpuncher never leads, but waits for the other fellow to lead and then ducks and counterpunches. For every blow that is aimed at him, he has a defense and then a quick counterpunch. There have been great fighters who are not punchers but counterpunchers. It's helpful to remember that the devil is a perfect counterpuncher.

No matter what a Christian tries to do, the devil blocks him and hits him a blow. Not a hard one, just enough to stun him a bit. Wherever you find the work of God going on, you will find the devil there, counterpunching, hitting back. He is not omnipresent, but he is ubiquitous. There is a difference. God is omnipresent; He is present everywhere, but the devil gets around so fast that it adds up to almost the same thing. Therefore, no matter where the work of God is going forward, you will find the devil there, blocking and countering and hindering.

In the Greek Olympic races, there was a scoundrel who would hide with a long javelin—a long lance. This fellow would hide behind a hedge somewhere, and as the racer raced by, he would throw that lance between the fellow's legs and tumble him over. By the time he got untangled, another runner was five miles down the road. The devil works that way. That scoundrel in the Olympic Games was called Diabolos, and they put that name right onto the devil, which is the way he works. When a child of God is running a holy race, Satan is blocking him or tripping him so that he falls.

Then another name for the devil is Satan. As Satan, he is the accuser of the brethren and tries to destroy his reputation before God and before men. Whenever a man's reputation is torn down, you may be sure who did it. Whatever agent he may have used, or whatever old gossip he may have gotten into, he is the author of it. So, we have this god of the world—a serpent, the dragon, the devil and Satan.

Unmortified Flesh

The flesh is with us always, and unless conquered on a daily basis, it will bring nothing but trouble. You cannot compromise with unmortified (unsubdued) flesh. It will always win out in the end.

This unmortified flesh will wear us down until we are utterly exhausted and finally give in to its desires. The only way to deal with this is to crucify it—bring it to the cross of Jesus—a radical act on our part. Those who try to negotiate with the flesh and make some sort of deal with it usually end up the loser. The difficulty with this area of danger is that it is a daily occurrence. It is not something that can be dealt with today and forgotten. The flesh is with us on a daily basis, and if we are not careful and if we do not realize the ultimate danger, it will rule our day.

The general rule in this area is to deal with the flesh, or the flesh will deal with you and it will not be nice.

These sources of danger—the world, the devil and our flesh—are very real. The danger is not imaginary, and only the reckless will ignore it. If you are a serious minded Christian, you will not take this as just one more warning. The wise want to know where the dangers are and what they are and how they can recognize them and overcome them.

David said, "the LORD is my rock, and my fortress, and my deliverer" (Ps. 18:2). He had to have help, so he said, "I will call upon the LORD, who is worthy to be praised: so shall I be saved from mine enemies" (v. 3). He said, "[God] sent from above, he took me, he drew me out of many waters. He delivered me from my strong enemy, and from them which hated me: for they were too strong for me. . . . He brought me forth also into a large place; he delivered me, because he delighted in me" (vv. 16-17,19).

I believe that deliverance is not only possible, but it is also normal for the child of God, if we have our eyes open. God does not want us to walk around with our eyes closed. If our eyes are open, we do not need to be struck down; we do not need to fall.

No matter what direction, no matter what the enemies are, we have David's God for our help. If we will call upon the Lord and cry unto Him, He will hear us from His holy temple and will send from above, take us and deliver us out of many waters, and deliver us because He delights in us.

Never has there been a time when I felt God's people should be more optimistic than now. Never a time when I felt they should be more encouraged in God than right now. We are living in wild, turbulent, dangerous, dramatic days, and the four winds are striving on the great sea, and the moon is mourning the time when it shall be turned to blood; but you and I need not fear. God is on our side, and God is on His holy throne and in His holy temple, and all is right with the man or woman who dares to believe.

Rock of Ages, Cleft for Me
Augustus M. Toplady (1740–1778)

Rock of Ages, cleft for me,
let me hide myself in thee;
let the water and the blood,
from thy wounded side which flowed,
be of sin the double cure;
save from wrath and make me pure.

Not the labors of my hands
can fulfill thy law's commands;
could my zeal no respite know,
could my tears forever flow,
all for sin could not atone;
thou must save, and thou alone.

Nothing in my hand I bring,
simply to the cross I cling;
naked, come to thee for dress;
helpless, look to thee for grace;
foul, I to the fountain fly;
wash me, Savior, or I die.

While I draw this fleeting breath,
when mine eyes shall close in death,
when I soar to worlds unknown,
see thee on thy judgment throne,
Rock of Ages, cleft for me,
let me hide myself in thee.

8

THE DANGER OF VICTORY AND DEFEAT

For a just man falleth seven times,
and riseth up again:
but the wicked shall fall into mischief.

PROVERBS 24:16

Many Christians have bought into the philosophy of victory at all costs. Whatever it takes to become victorious must be okay. Then, people who illustrate this brand of victory are paraded before us enough to make us ashamed of any failures we might have in life. According to the experts, life is one long string of victory after victory.

The problem with this is that nobody has ever experienced a life of absolute victory, without any defeat, except our Lord Himself. Even the expectation of victory can sometimes create a spirit of defeat in our hearts. This is one of the dangers facing the spiritually lethargic, and nobody seems to be pointing it out. Without knowing the dangers associated with victory, many have eagerly come to worship at its altar.

Let me simply say that our victory can spoil us, and our defeat can destroy us.

The Danger of Victory

Victory is certainly one of the goals in the Christian life, but whose definition of victory are we using? We strive to live the victorious Christian life, but who is telling us what that really is? We must vigorously search the Scriptures to discover God's definition of the victorious Christian life and then commit ourselves to that. No other definition is acceptable to the Christian. Because this is so utterly important, we must not misunderstand what victory is all about.

Let me point out that the victorious Christian life is not a life absent of any problems or difficulties or failures. Actually, the opposite is true. The victorious Christian life is a day-to-day or even moment-by-moment victory over enemies and situations that we confront in the way. That is why the man of God said, "For a just man falleth seven times." We are sometimes given the idea that a "just man" never falls at all. Because of that, we face the danger of arrogance.

Arrogance is the sin that follows in the wake of success. I have seen a few people who have bought their way through life and boss everybody around. They had the money to pay for it, and so the maid and the gardener and everybody else became a slave.

I once called a famous preacher to invite him to come and preach at our church. I could not even reach him. The secretary said he was busy and could not talk to me. It was a good many years ago, and I do not know whether he would talk to me now or not in a condescending attitude to my advancing years. The Lord will always punish us for that kind of thing, because He will never let you have a condescending attitude toward anybody else if you are a Christian. If you are a Christian, the Lord loves you too much to let you get away with that. Arrogance comes on the heels of victory.

Our Lord once rode into Jerusalem on Palm Sunday. He was a carpenter's son, they thought. He was not brought up in the schools. He did not know or use the jargon of the learned halls. He spoke the plain language of the Jerusalem streets.

As Jesus rode down the streets of Jerusalem, with everybody hailing Him and shouting, "Hosanna to the son of David: Blessed is he that cometh in the name of the LORD" (Matt. 21:9), it would have been a good opportunity to harbor thoughts of success and victory. That would have been the place for Jesus suddenly to say, "Maybe the devil was right. Maybe I can be king of the world. Maybe my friends who wanted me to be king were right about this."

It is always a temptation to let your victories get blown all out of proportion and give you a wrong concept of who you really are. Watch out for a reputation that is lauded. It is too easy to believe what people are saying about you. Jesus would not allow any success of any kind to lead Him astray. He knew the direction He was going and kept to that with all haste. Watch out if you get established and accepted in your field as being a victorious and successful person; when that happens, you are in danger. If, in your Christian life, you make some strides forward, you are in danger.

The same multitude that said "Hosanna," said, "Crucify Him." So keep that in mind. The great politician today can be in jail tomorrow. The crowd that thinks you are worthy of acclaim today may turn their backs on you tomorrow.

The Danger of Defeat or Failure

The danger of defeat is the opposite of the danger of victory. Remember the famous battle Israel fought at the walls of Jericho, and how the walls came tumbling down? Israel grew overconfident and thought she was doing it all, and went out to Ai.

They only took a few thousand along and said, "Ah, look what we did to Jericho," when all they did was shout and blow the ram's horn. God had done it all, but they thought they had done it themselves.

They must have thought the wind from the horns blew the wall down. At the next battle, they said, "Oh, we'll take Ai. No problem." They boasted arrogantly, "Boy, we're really in high gear now, and nothing generates success like success, and we'll take Ai the same as we took Jericho." They went out with their chests and their heads held high, but they soon fled ignominiously before those of Ai, and 35,000 died. Their defeat followed their victory, as effect follows cause.

The danger of victory is that it develops within us an arrogant spirit and we think we are invincible. Then the inevitable happens. Suddenly we are plunged into failure, which creates within us a spirit of discouragement often leading to a disheartenment. The old Shakespearean expression "he hath no stomach for it" means that a person does not have any zeal for that job; he does not like it. Loss of stomach, or discouragement, is like a sick person who has completely lost his appetite.

In the kingdom of God, a defeat or two of good hard reversal often drives us to the place where we have no stomach for anything. We pray but we have no stomach for it. We take it like food, but we do not enjoy it. We go to church, but we do not care for the church. Nothing means anything to us. Hymns are dull and tasteless; sermons are a bore; the whole thing is tasteless because we have lost our stomach. We are disheartened and are discouraged.

Many of God's people have experienced this. They have not lost eternal life, and their relation to God has not changed. They are still His children and Christ is still pleading their cause at the right hand of the Father. Heaven is still their home, but for the time being, they have lost their stomach for it. They have no appetite; they have been defeated, and so defeatism has hold of them. I have gone into churches where it was obvious that nobody expected anything to happen, and the result, of course, is what you would expect . . . nothing.

There is a real danger in defeat. Suppose a man were to slip and fall on an icy sidewalk and say, "I don't suppose there's any use for me to try it again." He would finally struggle to his feet, go another block, fall again, and then say, "I know something's seriously wrong with my equilibrium, and I'll have to accept that I can never can walk upright again on ice." Of course, he would have to go to bed too. That is defeatism; it is allowing a defeat to put a permanent reversal in your heart.

At one conference I attended, I walked by a porch where a young preacher sat. He was a fine-looking young fellow, but that morning his chin was just about reaching the ground. I started teasing him a bit and gave him a nice pleasantry, with no response. He did not smile or respond except to say, "Mr. Tozer, something awful has happened to me."

I said, "What's the matter now? What's happened to you?"

"I just took my examination for ordination and I flunked it," he said. "I've flunked my examination, and they won't ordain me."

I knew what this young man was going through, and he was in danger of developing a real spirit of defeatism. So I set about to encourage him and change his disposition a little. I said, "Abraham Lincoln was defeated twice before he was elected. If God has called you, go to your examining board and find out what you did not know. Buy some books and study up on it and ask for another examination."

His chin came up and he said, "Is this what you suggest?"

I said, "Sure, don't let a little thing like this get you down. If God has called you, He is not withdrawing the call because of some questions you could not answer. Study up on it, find out what the trouble is, bore into the book, get hold of it, pray and ask God to help you; the next time, you will go through all right."

That is exactly what happened. He became a successful young pastor and got along fine. However, if somebody had not come along to encourage him, it might have been the end for him. He probably would have got in his car and gone home and said, "There's no use. God has let me down, the Spirit's deserted me, and I don't even know enough to pass an examination."

Suppose you pray for something and do not get it, and it is obvious that you are not going to get it. Do not let that finish you off. Maybe you are not living right; maybe you are praying selfishly; maybe you have misunderstood the will of God. Go to the Scriptures, search it out, get right with God, give God a chance at you, then try it again and press on. Finally, the Lord will either tell you to hold on, or that you are praying for the wrong thing and to pray for this thing and He will give it to you; or else He will give you what you prayed for the first time. But do not stay defeated.

Rules to Get Through Victory or Defeat

I have trained myself by the Word of God and prayer never to look that way at things. I am to take God's side, the resurrection side, the victory side, and live on that side of things. Let me set before you four rules to help you get through either victory or defeat.

Do Not Trust a Discouraged Heart

Never trust your heart when you are feeling discouraged or, for that matter, when you have just won a great victory. If you are in the throes of a horrible defeat, simply quiet your heart and make no decisions. Remember, this too shall pass.

If you are a Christian, the Holy Spirit dwells in some measure in you, and He has not turned you away. If everybody else thinks you are not so good in your profession; if your voice is not quite as glorious as you would like to think it is; if maybe your brains and wisdom are not as great as you'd like to think they are; if somebody has got the news and passed it around to you through the grapevine and you have heard it and are blue, let them think it of you.

A discouraged heart always exaggerates everything. Do not trust a discouraged spirit, for it will never give you the true picture of you or your situation.

Postpone Any Immediate Decision-making

Not many things need to be decided right on the spot. Give yourself time. There is not a pastor anywhere that has not, at some time, written out his resignation on Saturday and then on Sunday the blessing came, and he tore it up. Do not write out your resignation when you are discouraged. Do not resign from anything when you are discouraged. When you are down and blue, do not make a move.

Many people have, at a moment of deep discouragement, resigned or quit or moved and lived to regret it. Many other people have gone through the "slough of despondency" and held on until they were through it and broke into the marvelous sunlight of God's delight.

Every decision for the Lord has the right moment. To make that decision prematurely is often to miss the blessing of God. When you are on top of the world, and you say, "I can do all things through Christ when strengtheneth me" (Phil. 4:13), then make your decision.

Reflect on Your Relationship with God

Regardless of your victory or failure, your relationship with God does not change. You are no less dear to God when you are a failure than when you are successful.

Your relationship with others may change, depending upon your status of victory or defeat, but it never changes with God. I can endure the distrust of my friends, but I cannot endure God thinking little of me. As I peruse the Scriptures, I discover, much to my delight, that God thinks the world of me. I am his child. Even though I make mistakes and stumble, I am still a child of the living God. He looks down on me with a bright smile of grace and mercy. I am the apple of His adoring eye.

Saturate Yourself with God's Promises

Time alone with God, with an open Bible, can change a heart filled with defeat into a heart rejoicing in the unchangeable promises of God. God's Word never changes, regardless of our success or failure. God is your rock, your fortress, your deliverer, your buckler, your strength and your high tower. He sent from above, took you, and drew you out of many waters. He delivered you from your strong enemy and from them that hated you. He brought you forth to a large place, and He delivered you because He delighted in you (see Ps. 18:16-19).

We Are on God's Side

I have a little verse I have loved for years: "For thou wilt light my candle: the LORD my God will enlighten my darkness" (Ps. 18:28). Maybe the little candle has gone out. Well, God will light our candle for us. He will light it and He will enlighten our darkness. Believe it.

God is our refuge, and we are not going to let victory spoil us, nor will we allow defeat dishearten us. We are going to take it all in stride. Win or lose, we are on God's side; and if we keep away from sin and keep above it all and keep happy in God, we are winning whether we know it or not. We can be just as happy when we are not happy as we are when we are happy, because that is the prerogative of living the life of faith.

On to Victory
Elisha A. Hoffman (1839–1929)

Christian, gird the armor on,
There's a vict'ry to be won
For the Lord, for the Lord;
Take the helmet, sword, and shield,
Forth unto the battlefield
At His Word, at His Word.

Let His banner be unfurled,
Till it waves o'er all the world,
Sea to sea, shore to shore;
Till the nations all shall own
He is King, and He alone,
Evermore, evermore.

When the battle shall be done,
And the victory be won
Conflict past, conflict past;
In our happy home above,
We'll receive a crown of love,
At the last, at the last.

That will be an hour of joy,
Praise shall then our tongues employ
More and more, more and more;

We shall stand before the King,
And the song of triumph sing
Evermore, evermore.

On we'll march to victory;
Jesus will our leader be,
Jesus will our leader be;
On we'll march to victory,
To a final and a glorious victory.

9

THE DANGER OF BONDAGE AND LIBERTY

Stand fast therefore in the liberty wherewith Christ hath made us free, and be not entangled again with the yoke of bondage.

GALATIANS 5:1

The apostle Paul says that we are to be careful and not return to the yoke of bondage from which we were once delivered. This bondage can be expressed in superstition and legalistic forms and externals such as food, dress and bondage to holy days and seasons.

Bondage to Superstition

Superstition is something American people laugh about in public. Superstition is commonly referred to as "an abject attitude of mind toward nature founded upon ignorance." It is a belief in magic and chance. Some believe—anthropologists and those who follow their beliefs—that returning to primitive conditions is the hope of the world. They say, "Why do you go into the Baliem Valley in Papua? Why don't you let them alone? You will merely take to them the common cold, tooth decay, bad digestion and all other of the white man's curses. Why don't you leave them in their simple childlike beauty?"

Talk like that is completely out of touch with reality. Ask any missionary whether there is such a tribe on the face of the earth. There is none. Superstition rides the primitive peoples of the world like an iron yoke. It keeps them in constant bondage, as if they were wearing a ball and chain. They are afraid of everything—the sun, the stars at night, an eclipse, the wind, the cry of the night bird. They live in a state of trembling terror at what they do not understand. When twins are born in some parts of the primitive world, they save the first twin because they say God sent that one, but take the second one out and kill it. It is a child of the devil.

Superstition is not found only in primitive societies; it is found wherever men are found. It may be refined, and some of the grosser manifestations are not present, but most people are superstitious. In the part of the country where I came from, superstition rested upon the shoulders of the simple country people and rode them all their lives.

Superstition Defames God's Character

Superstition is not something to joke about. It is a specific defamation of the character of God. Superstition assumes, without knowing it, that God is weak and cannot control things. Fear of devils and combinations of numbers and certain days and stars and the constellations and certain combinations of star patterns assume that God created a juggernaut in this world, which He cannot control. The universe is too big for Him, and He moves about and nervously hurries here and there through His universe.

The superstitious man pictures a limited god who created a universe over which he cannot have full control. Therefore, witches, spells, incantations, devils, demons, omens and the rest roam up and down the earth, and god hides in some cosmic closet, afraid of what he has created; that is defamation of the divine character.

Superstition casts aspersions upon the wisdom of God, assuming that God is limited and can be fooled and cheated like any common Roman god. Whereas, God knows all things, and our thoughts are loud to Him. He can hear the tiniest thought that lies in the back of your mind, infinitely amplified, and He knows it before you entertain it.

God cannot be fooled. He knows what is in man. He looks on the inside; He predicts and predestinates, and He is not limited in any sense and knowledge. There is no such thing as cheating God. No such thing as making God a promise and then having God wring His hands and say, "Why, that man broke his promise to me! Whatever shall I do?" That kind of God would never get my loyalty. Never would I bow my knee to a god that I could cheat. Never would I worship and cry, "Holy, holy, holy," in the presence of a god I could lie to successfully.

Superstition makes God limited in power and wisdom, or it shows Him to be spiteful so that He takes childish revenge. Superstition is, in some measure, a projection of our own nasty little personalities into heaven and making God in our own image; when we attribute a vast and limitless spitefulness to God, people become afraid of Him.

God Is Infinitely Patient, Kind and Merciful

God is above spite, which is why He pays no attention to someone who gets up and says, "If there's a God, let Him strike me dead in 10 seconds." Ten awful seconds pass when scarcely the heart beats and nobody breathes, waiting for the spiteful God in heaven to strike him down. The superstitious are waiting for God to rise up and act like a man. God is not spiteful. God is infinitely patient with us poor little chest-beating boasters. He is infinitely kind and merciful. If He were not, we should all be in hell today.

Some fundamentalists are afraid to say anything not exactly the right formula, lest the God who goes in big for words and syllables should be angry. Some never pronounce the name of Jesus apart from all of His titles. Lord Jesus Christ, Jesus Christ the Lord, or Christ Jesus the Lord, always they must have the three, as a poor, cheap preacher who's been given an honorary degree and is jealous to be called Doctor. They must feel that Jesus is jealous of all of His titles and that He gets miffed unless we give Him all His titles every time we speak about Him. What kind of a Christ would that be? A childish, churlish Christ that you never know exactly how to predict.

Superstition within a man makes God to be little and childish; makes Him to be limited or weak, whereas, He is none of these things. I think we could metaphorically throw out carload after carload of shackles to be melted up into soft metal and made into useful things, if we could only believe in the greatness of God and see how big and glorious, sovereign, mighty, patient, loving and holy God is.

All weaknesses in the Body of Christ spring out of an inadequate view of God. They spring out of a low view of God. If God were seen as big enough, there would be a wonderful liberty in the Church.

Bondage to Legalistic Forms

Some Christians cannot worship unless they worship after a certain form. If they were brought up to kneel, they cannot pray standing up. If they were brought up to pray standing up, they cannot pray lying down. They just have to get into that certain formula—form and posture, and say certain words. They that worship God must worship Him how? In spirit and in truth, and that gives us complete liberty. "Now the Lord is that Spirit: and where the Spirit of the Lord is, there is liberty" (2 Cor. 3:17). The child of God has infinite liberty in worshiping God.

We do not practice our religion as a witch practices her formula. We worship God spontaneously, out of our heart. We love Him, He loves us; there is no form there. Although there must be some form in public worship, otherwise it would be bedlam. Somebody needs to know what we are going to sing next, and so on, so I believe in a limited modified form in church service. It is possible to get so legalistic and into such bondage and formality that you will blow up in a fit of temper if things are not done the way they should be done in church.

Bondage to Traditions

Then there are the traditions, which may not go back to Christ and the apostles at all. It is possible to follow certain mannerisms or forms—traditions—and not know where they originated or how they got there, and yet they are religiously followed and imitated by all aspiring Christians.

Walter Post, a missionary in the Netherlands East Indies (now Indonesia), heard a young converted Dyack preaching. He was quite a preacher and could declare the Word of God in the language of his people wonderfully. Michelson, another missionary there, told me afterward, "This young Dyack preacher was a great preacher, but he had a peculiar mannerism. He would pull at his collar while he preached, and reach for his collar and pull at it, then reach with the other hand and pluck at his collar. I did not understand why he did it until I heard Walter preach. He pulled at his collar, and I didn't know why Walter did it until I came home and heard you [Tozer], and you plucked at your collar."

That kind of thing sounds silly, but it's possible to get into bondage to a thing, carry it down the years, found churches upon it and get your soul into a straitjacket. Throw your shoulders back, breathe deep and say, "In Jesus Christ, I'm a free man, and I will not be subject to bondage of any kind."

Bondage to Food and Clothing

Another type of bondage to watch out for is the bondage to foods and to dress. Jesus said it did not matter what entered into a man's mouth, that did not defile him; but it was what came out of the man's mouth that defiled him (see Matt. 15:17-20). Paul said that in the latter days, certain men would come and they would give heed to doctrines of devils (see 1 Tim. 4:1). The doctrines of devils were that they should not marry and that they should abstain from meat, which God had created to be received with thanksgiving by all that know and believe the truth. For all the gifts of God are good. All creatures are good and are to be received with thanksgiving, for the Word of God and prayer sanctify it.

There is certainly an emancipation proclamation that delivers you from foods, and yet in spite of that, we find many of God's dear children running back in and taking the oath; they do not feel comfortable without it. Like the man who used the crutch so long that now he feels naked when he does not use his crutch. There are people like that; they must have something to make them miserable. They just will not be free in God, so they will not eat or they will eat that, and they buy a book somewhere to show them why they are right scientifically.

The rule is that if it does not hurt you, eat it if you can afford it. If you do not have an allergy to it, go ahead and eat it, because all creatures of God are good and are to be received with thanksgiving to them that believe and know the truth. If you break out in a rash, do not eat it; but if you do not break out, go ahead and eat it. Do not think there is any such thing as religious food. No food is more religious than any other food: "But meat commendeth us not to God: for neither, if we eat, are we the better; neither, if we eat not, are we the worse" (1 Cor. 8:8). That ought to take care of that.

Spirituality does not lie in the length of your hair or the length of your beard. It does not lie in the style of your garment or the quality of your garment. The rule I would lay down is the easiest rule in the world: If it is modest and you can afford it, it is appropriate. That is all God cares about dress.

Bondage to Days and Seasons

How the churches are filled on Easter, and how empty they are the next Sunday, which all goes to show that such Christians are bound if they are Christians at all. When should we worship? Saturday, or Sunday? Some say one day; some say another. Those who worship on Saturday would not be caught dead in some church on a Sunday. Moreover, those who worship on Sunday certainly would not be caught dead in church on a Saturday. Isn't it strange that Christ died on the cross in order for us to argue on which day of the week we are to worship Him?

Then there are the holy days. Some celebrate them all, and some celebrate none. It is possible to be so bound to a church calendar that we lose sight of what it really means to be a Christian and have our sins washed in the blood of the Lamb. The worst bondage would be to insist that someone else bear the same bondage you do. Do not get into bondage to anything. Jesus Christ set us free to do His will.

The Danger of Taking Liberty Too Far

Antinomianism is a long, jaw-breaking word that means that certain people tend to run unchecked logic to extremes. If I get up and say, "You are free," they immediately leap into the air and say, "Thank God, I'm free. I'll do as I please," and they go out and commit sin to show how free they are.

Paul said, "For, brethren, ye have been called unto liberty; only use not liberty for an occasion to the flesh, but by love serve one another" (Gal. 5:13). God set us free, but He did not set us free to do evil. He set us free to do good. Freedom to do good is the Christian's liberty. God never said, "You're free now, go out and sin." Some Christians have carried freedom to such a ridiculous and unholy extreme, they say, "I've got to sin a little to keep grace operating." I think that is a tragic heresy, and the children of God should know it for such and flee it as they would some contagious disease.

True Christian Liberty

Christian liberty is freedom to live in the Spirit, unhindered by externals. Christian liberty is freedom from the fear of the government, freedom from fear of your sins, freedom from fear of God's service, freedom from fear of the devil, freedom from black cats and birds and amulets and spells and charms and wizardry, freedom from religious bondage of every kind, and freedom from the iron yoke of traditions. Christian liberty is freedom to live in the Spirit and worship God in spirit and in truth. When it becomes freedom to commit sin so that "grace may abound," Paul cried out against it and shouted, "God forbid. How shall we, that are dead to sin, live any longer therein?" (Rom. 6:1-2).

We have freedom to love, so our conduct springs out of love and the freedom not to hate. It is wonderful to be free from hate. Hate is a moral cancer and eats on the soul until it kills the victim. To get free from hatred is like being healed of cancer. Freedom from hatred, from envy, from unholy ambition, from wanting your own way, and the freedom to do the will of God is Christian freedom; that is true Christian liberty. Christian liberty is never about the freedom to commit any sort of sin. The child of God who lives from within and whose heart is a fountain of affection and love for God will not sin; but if he does, he will confess it with sorrow and be forgiven and cleansed from it and determine not to go back to that wallow anymore.

Christian Liberty's Affect on Others

A Christian will never use his freedom to put other Christians into bad conscience. Paul told about meat offered to idols, and some Christians had a conscience about it. In 1 Corinthians 8, Paul said, in effect, "I have no conscience at all about meat that has been offered to an idol, if it's good clean meat. Because I do not believe an idol is a real thing. There is one God, one Lord, one Spirit and all these other so-called gods are all imitations. They don't exist for me."

"Yet," said Paul, "when I'm in the home of the young Christian that doesn't know this, I'll respectfully pass on meat offered to idols, lest I hurt his conscience." Therefore, a Christian is in danger of allowing his very liberty to be a stumbling block to somebody else, so that he does freely things that other people will think he is sinning when he does; and thus he is a hindrance to other people.

A rule I go by is to be as free in Christ as He made you. Remember, you are not a bondslave, but a son. You are not a servant in the house; you are a child in the household. You are your Father's child. Be free, but do not use your freedom as a license to the flesh. Mortify the flesh and keep your flesh subdued, and lay loving burdens on yourself, for Christ's sake. A burden I voluntarily lay upon my shoulder is no burden at all.

His Burden Is Light

What you do voluntarily is not a burden, it is only a yoke when somebody else lays it on your neck and says, "Wear this yoke or perish." If somebody with a beard or clothing of a certain kind, or a tradition behind him, or some other religious accouterments to add to his personality and take authority he does not have, I smile—I hope not superciliously—and tell him, "Oh, friend, you don't know my Father. My Father does not look at it that way. My Father says 'Child, you're free; absolutely free. Free to take voluntary burdens for the sake of others. Carry those burdens on your shoulder and the burden you carry voluntarily will never make your shoulders sore. The burden that religion lays upon you or philosophy or tradition or superstition will gall you and scar you and kill you at last. However, the yoke of Jesus is easy and His burden is light.'"

The Lord Jesus has never asked a hard thing of me. My miseries have always come out of my own flesh, never from any burden Jesus ever laid on me. What few burdens I have laid on myself for Jesus' sake, I have never felt the weight of them at all. They are as easy and light as can be.

So let us watch and not become bound to anything, for we are free men and women in Christ Jesus. Let us be sensible and not use our freedom as a cloak for the flesh; and let us not hide behind liberty in order to practice license. Let us remember that the man in whom Jesus Christ dwells ought to be a good man. Do not be afraid of the word "good." Let us not fling back in the face of Jesus the charter of freedom that cost Him His blood. Stand fast therefore in the liberty wherewith Christ has made you free and be not entangled with the yoke of bondage, but use not your freedom as a cloak for the flesh (see Gal. 5:1,13).

Knowing that you are free, discipline yourself for Jesus' sake and trust the indwelling Spirit to fulfill in you the law of

God. For what the law could not do in that it was weak through the flesh, God's sending His Son has done by the indwelling Spirit within us.

Jesus Only
Ralph E. Hudson (1842–1901)

Jesus only, when the sinful heart
Would lay its burden down;
Jesus only takes the weary load
And bears it as His own.

Jesus only, Jesus only,
From the cradle to the grave;
Jesus only, Jesus only,
For no other name can save.

Jesus only helps the wayward feet
To keep the narrow way;
Jesus only guides the wav'ring soul,
Lest it in sin should stray.

Jesus only, when the weary one
May lay the armor down;
Jesus only takes the heavy cross,
And gives the shining crown.

Jesus only, when the ransomed soul
Has reached the "Golden shore!"
Jesus only, this shall be my song,
Forever, evermore.

10

THE DANGER OF IDLENESS AND BUSYNESS

See then that ye walk circumspectly, not as fools, but as wise.

EPHESIANS 5:15

The farmer who never observes the wind or looks at the clouds will be a foolish farmer and will not have a successful crop at the end of the year. On the other hand, the man who becomes so cloud and wind conscious that he gets up and moistens his finger and holds it up to see which way the wind is blowing every morning, and then sneaks back if there's a cloud overhead, will get nothing done. There will always be a cloud warning you to stay indoors; the wise man will know which cloud to regard and which to disregard.

My intention is not to make anybody merely danger conscious. If you become excessively danger conscious, it will slow you down. The Scripture says, "He that observeth the wind shall not sow; and he that regardeth the clouds shall not reap" (Eccles. 11:4). Christians are not to become so conscious of the wind and the clouds that they do nothing. On the other hand, if we are unaware of danger, we increase that danger a hundred-fold and almost guarantee disaster.

The Danger of Idleness

There is a notion abroad that labor is a sin or, at best, a curse resting upon us. Some Christians even have the notion that work is a disciplinary punishment, which the Lord laid upon the world at the Fall. Nothing could be further from the fact. Read the Bible before the third chapter of Genesis and the Fall, and you will see that God told the newly created couple that they were to replenish the earth and subdue it.

Replenishing the earth meant there were to be children born into the world. Anybody who imagines there can be children brought up in the world without work has never had children or even been around them. The command to subdue the earth certainly embraces the idea of work.

Labor and Subdue the Earth

Then it says that they were placed in a garden to dress it and to keep it. They were not there to be idle. God the Creator made man in His image and made him to be something of a creator too. Man was to labor and subdue the earth and bring children into the world and work to bring up those children. The man and the woman were to dress the garden and keep it in shape, so that meant work.

Work is not a result of the Fall, but sin did bring sorrow, thorns, thistles and sweat. Those four words did not occur in the first and second chapters of Genesis. There was no "sorrow," "thorns," "thistle" and "sweat." But the word "work" or its equivalent occurred: "Dress" and "keep" and "subdue" and "care" were used in Genesis 1 and 2.

The words "sorrow," "thorns," "thistles" and "sweat" were added when man sinned. Work is not a result of man's sin; working in sorrow is a result of man's sin. To work with thorns and thistles around you is the result of man's sin. To work until we sweat for our daily labor is a result of man's sin. God made us to be workers. Idleness is un-Christlike—our Savior was a worker—and contrary to the high will of God, for it voids our commission to replenish the earth and subdue it, and it is an invitation to temptation. Isaac Watts (1674–1748) wrote the following in *Against Idleness and Mischief*, his little book for children:

> In works of labour, or of skill,
>   I would be busy too;
> For Satan finds some mischief still
>   For idle hands to do.

The word "idle" was, in other days, an evil word. Our fathers scorned the word and understood that the devil always finds some task for idle hands to do.

I think it would be safe to say that people who have nothing to do are responsible for most of the deviltry in the world. People who are engaged in some kind of productive activity may sin, but they are not as likely to as those who have nothing to do. It was when King David had avoided his duties during the season of war, and was on the housetop taking a little idle walk, that he looked down and saw the scene that led him to the great temptation into adultery and murder.

The idle Christian is in great danger, because he is unlike his Savior. Our Lord went about doing good, and He chose industrious men for His disciples. He did not go to the Riviera and pick playboys. He picked simple men who were hard workers, who took an interest in life and had something to do. He did it deliberately and purposefully.

Get Something Done

God made us for creative activity. If you want to live closer to the way that God commissioned you in the book of Genesis, I recommend you make yourself available—that you be ready to do anything. Do not hold yourself back until you feel ready to do something. Start doing something now that you have wanted to do but put off. Learn to ride a bicycle by trial and error. Do not wait until you have learned to ride it before you buy one; get one now and practice on it. Get something done. You may make mistakes at first, of course, but do something.

Some people say there is nothing for them to do around the Church. The Church has a wealth of talent and there is nothing for them to do. I suppose that person would mean that there is already a soloist, or there is no committee to be chairman of. If it has to be chairman of a committee or singing solos, the average church would not have room for everybody. But any Christian worth his salt will find something to do in the kingdom of God.

Christians are like farm implements. Farm machinery seldom wears out. If you keep your machinery up, you can use it summer in and summer out until it becomes obsolete. The idle machine sitting in the dampness will go to pieces in one season, but that same machine used for 10 years will only make it shine.

One year of sitting around sulking will do more to rust your soul than 100 years of hard work, if God granted you that many years. Do not fear wearing yourself out. The devil is a master of strategy, and when a child of God gets busy, he whispers in the ear, "Watch it, because you're going to have a nervous breakdown." I am positively sure that nervous breakdowns do not come from working in the easy yoke of Jesus Christ. They come from frustrations, hidden sins, stubbornness, refusing to hear God and wanting your own way; but they do not come from working. "My yoke is easy, and my burden is light" (Matt. 11:30).

Not a gray hair in this head of mine was ever placed there by honest labor in the kingdom of my Savior. How many are there because I wanted my own way or because I wanted the world to obey me, and it would not listen? Stubbornness, contrariness and resentfulness—those will bring frustration and illness, but not the legwork of the Lord. Jesus Christ would never have gotten sick. He could have lived an infinite number of years working as He worked. He did not kill Himself by hard work; they had to kill Him on a cross. Paul became old in the work of God, and He was still going when they cut off his head. Peter, when they crucified him, was still in the spiritual harness of labor.

Working in the Service of the Lord

Our human weaknesses and faults cause us to break down, and we end up not working the service of the Lord. Do not be afraid to work. It may be too late to do much now with your time. The rust is so complete that with one good lunge you are finished. I do not think it is true of very many, and maybe it's not true of anybody. I am optimistic enough to think that there may be a little rust around here and there, but you can get rid of that by going to work. You can wear your rust off easy, and you will not wear yourself out in doing it.

There is plenty of work in the Church. There is intercession to be made. There are calls to be made. There are letters to be written. There are booklets and tracts to be distributed. There is singing to be done. There are children and youth to encourage. There are many things to be done.

Years ago, in Indianapolis, a man asked me whether he could do something around the church. I said, "I don't know anything you can do." I thought he wanted to be chairman of something, but he did not. He said, "Can I take care of the lawn?" I said, "Yes, you can take care of the lawn."

That lawn and the grounds never prospered as much as they did under his care. He varnished the sign out in front; he kept the little fence up nicely; and the lawn began to look like a golf course. This man had only been converted for a short time, but something ordained of God in him wanted to work. He was humble enough that he was willing to take care of a lawn—anything to look after the work of God and do something.

It was not long until he was preaching on the street. After that, he began preaching in institutions here and there. It was not long before he began to go to another town out from Indianapolis and hold meetings. Eventually, that formed into a little group. Now there is a church there, preaching the gospel, giving to missions, praying for missions and sending out missionaries—all because one man, newly converted, was willing to do anything for the Lord.

If he had sobbed and told his wife, "There's too much talent around here. I can't be chairman of anything. I have nothing to do," he would have rusted out and that church outside of Indianapolis never would have been established. He was too much of a Christian to want to head something, but he began by cutting the church lawn.

The devil always finds something for idle men and women to do. There is a danger in idleness. So let us walk circumspectly and not be idle.

The Danger of Busyness

Idleness is a ditch on one side of the road, but over on the other side is another ditch called busyness. There is a great danger in busyness. Solomon wrote:

> To everything there is a season, and a time to every purpose under the heaven: A time to be born, and a time to

die; and a time to plant, and a time to pluck up that which is planted; a time to kill, and a time to heal; a time to break down, and a time to build up; A time to weep, and a time to laugh; a time to mourn, and a time to dance; a time to cast away stones, and a time to gather stones together; a time to embrace, and a time to refrain from embracing; a time to get, and a time to lose; a time to keep, and a time to cast away; a time to rend, and a time to sew; a time to keep silence, and a time to speak (Eccles. 3:1-7).

A wise Christian realizes that he is not to be extreme on anything, but he is to know the time and the season. The Scripture in Ecclesiastes does not say there is a time for idleness, but there is a time for relaxation. There is a time to realize that it is time to camp—that you pitch your tent and do not go on for that day. You have gone far enough that day.

There is no time for idleness, because idleness assumes lack of purpose. If I have no purpose, I will be idle. Idleness assumes disinclination to be inconvenienced and it assumes addiction to pleasures. We have so many gadgets today that minister to idleness. There is no place for that in the kingdom of God, but there is a time to cease activities. Even the creatures beside the fire up in the heaven, as revealed in the first chapter of Ezekiel, tell us that those creatures let down their wings and waited on God (see Ezek. 1:25).

It is possible that we are so busy in our secular work or even in the Lord's work that we have no time to pray—no time to wait on God, or get still and knit up the raveled sleeve of care, or orient our souls toward God in heaven. When that happens, there is danger. Daniel prayed three times a day; the prophets sought the silence. You will find that God looked for His men in the silence. Men who cannot be silent will not say anything when they talk. It is only out of the silence that the Word speaks. In the beginning was silence, and then there was a word.

The idea was that God spoke out of the everlasting silence of His own holy self-contained being. We are likely to be so busy that we do not get anything done, and so talkative that we never say anything. The prophets sought the silence; and in the silence, they learned what to say. Then they broke the silence by saying it and relapsed back into the silence again. We could well cut down the decibels in our homes and in our churches.

I am always cautious and afraid of noisy people. It takes a very wise man to talk all the time and say anything of value. So let us learn the scriptural silence. Christ Himself went into the desert and there, in the silence of 40 days and nights, He waited on God, under the temptation of the devil. He came out from there in the fullness of the Spirit and went out to preach the Word of God everywhere. Our Lord Himself told us to shut the door. He said, "But thou, when thou prayest, enter into thy closet, and when thou hast shut thy door, pray to thy Father which is in secret; and thy Father which seeth in secret shall reward thee openly" (Matt. 6:6).

Cultivate Time with God

Secular business can ruin men. A man called me and said, "I have been a Christian a few years and I want to do God's will. I have a real estate business and have partners. We have made it a rule to be open only on weekdays and closed on Sundays. Now my partners want to open on Sunday. What would you say?"

I told him by all means follow the light. By all means lose the sale and keep your good conscience. If your partners will not listen, sell out and start something of your own. God will bless you for it.

I am not a Sabbatarian. I do not believe one day is above another day. But I believe we ought to have some time for God. The man who works seven days a week has no time for God, and the office that keeps open to get a few extra nickels on that seventh day has no time for God. Whether he takes Wednesday, Sunday or Friday off, he ought to take a day off; but Sunday would be the day to take off. It is a testimony and enables the man to get into the house of God and mingle and raise his voice in the songs of Zion with the people of God. We are not Sabbatarians, but we do believe that there is a time for everything, and secular business can ruin men, unless they take time to cultivate God.

Excessive religious work can do the same, unless we take time to cultivate God. Dr. R. A. Torrey knew that too much busyness in the work of the Lord can destroy the effectiveness of that work. He would take two weeks out of every year, put on old clothes and go into the hills. Nobody but his wife knew his whereabouts. And nothing short of a death was to get a message through to him. Two weeks he would wait, relax, rest, gaze at the sky, listen and then come back to the busy world with a heart and mind filled with truth. I want to give you a little motto: If you are too busy in the Lord's work to spend time in the Lord's presence, you are too busy in the Lord's work.

Let us be careful. Let us walk circumspectly, looking around. Here is the broad highway of God. Over on the left is idleness, and over on the right is excessive busyness; and then there is the great broad highway in the middle. We can follow that highway and go along and have plenty of room and get a world of work done and still not rust out from idleness or kill ourselves with excessive busyness. There is a time for everything. We wait on God to renew our batteries, and then when they are up to full power, we turn them loose into the work of God. Thus, we go, not as fools, but as wise men. Remember these two dangers. Woe to the idle Christian. He will not grow in grace.

Let us ask God for wisdom, not to be idle ever, but to be inactive sometimes, for the sake of renewing our batteries and relaxing our nerves and quieting our minds and, above all things, seeing visions of God. Then we will not fall into either ditch, but walk down the great broad highway of Zion toward a predetermined end.

Work, for the Night Is Coming
Anna L. Coghill (1836–1907)

Work, for the night is coming,
Work through the morning hours;
Work while the dew is sparkling,
Work 'mid springing flowers;

Work when the day grows brighter,
Work in the glowing sun;
Work, for the night is coming,
When man's work is done.

Work, for the night is coming,
Work through the sunny noon;
Fill brightest hours with labor,
Rest comes sure and soon.

Give every flying minute,
Something to keep in store;
Work, for the night is coming,
When man works no more.

Work, for the night is coming,
Under the sunset skies;
While their bright tints are glowing,
Work, for daylight flies.

Work till the last beam fadeth,
Fadeth to shine no more;
Work, while the night is darkening,
When man's work is o'er.

11

THE DANGER OF PROSPERITY AND ADVERSITY

*Two things have I required of thee; deny me them not before
I die: Remove far from me vanity and lies: give me neither poverty
nor riches; feed me with food convenient for me: Lest I be full,
and deny thee, and say, Who is the LORD? or lest I be poor, and steal,
and take the name of my God in vain.*

PROVERBS 30:7-9

Can you imagine how it would be if it were possible to sabotage this country all in one night, by taking down all highway markers from Maine to California, from the Gulf to the Canadian border? Not one left! Can you imagine how many thousands would be killed the next evening? Thousands would die because the signs that carefully marked the dangerous places were no longer there.

The idea is that when the dangers have been well marked, you do not have to stop and go back, and you don't have to drive all jittery and afraid, because the dangerous places are marked. If you pay attention to the markers and drive with some degree of relaxed care, the possibility of an accident will be cut down to an infinitesimal minimum. But if you pay no attention to the markers, or if the markers are removed, the danger is multiplied substantially.

To ignore or remove the markers on the highway of life is to do a dangerous disservice to the people of God. When a man rises and says, "I believe the Bible" and then ignores the teachings of the Bible on his own pet subjects, he is rejecting the Word more insidiously than outright disbelief. We are all likely to do that. I am likely to do it, and I pray that I may never do it, that I might be wise not to do it. Well-intentioned men, without meaning to ignore the Scriptures, do deny them. They have ignored the dangers in the Christian way, and so they have taken away the markers on the highways.

The Danger of Prosperity

It is a solemn thought that the history of humanity and of nations and of churches shows that we trust in God, as a rule, when there is nothing else in which to trust. A Christian ought to be a realist. That is, he ought to stay by the facts, as they are, not invent or twist them. The simple fact is that the history of men, Israel, the Church and the nations and of individual churches shows that we trust in God last. We tend to trust in God when we have nothing else in which to trust. As other things to trust in appear, we turn from God to them and excuse ourselves eloquently by saying that we are not trusting them, we are trusting God.

The Israelites used the very prosperity God had given them as a stumbling block. In Deuteronomy 32:17-20, we read the following:

> They sacrificed unto devils, not to God; to gods whom they knew not, to new gods that came newly up, whom your fathers feared not. Of the Rock that begat thee

thou art unmindful, and hast forgotten God that formed thee. And when the LORD saw it, he abhorred them, because of the provoking of his sons, and of his daughters. And he said, "I will hide my face from them, I will see what their end shall be: for they are a very froward generation, children in whom is no faith."

"Froward" means brazen, shameless, with a hard neck of brass—children in whom is no faith. These men would have made an eloquent defense of these gods. There would have been magazine articles and books written and committees formed. There would be a strong defense in favor of whatever is new and the fact that we must not miss the boat.

When we come to the New Testament, you would think humanity would have changed during the hundreds of years from about 1450 BC to AD 50 or so. In that 1,500 years, Christ came and died and ascended to the Father and sent the Holy Spirit, and the Church was formed. But see the words of Jesus that the apostle writes to a church in Laodicea:

And unto the angel of the church of the Laodiceans write; these things saith the Amen, the faithful and true witness, the beginning of the creation of God; I know thy works, that thou art neither cold nor hot: I would thou wert cold or hot. So then because thou art lukewarm, and neither cold nor hot, I will spue thee out of my mouth. Because thou sayest, I am rich, and increased with goods, and have need of nothing; and knowest not that thou art wretched, and miserable, and poor, and blind, and naked: I counsel thee to buy of me gold tried in the fire, that thou mayest be rich; and white raiment, that thou mayest be clothed, and that the shame of thy nakedness do not appear; and anoint thine eyes with eyesalve, that thou mayest see (Rev. 3:14-18).

In case you think this is severe, notice that Christ said, "As many as I love, I rebuke and chasten: be zealous therefore, and repent. Behold, I stand at the door, and knock" (vv. 19-20). This pitiful condition of the rich Church in the latter days—increased with goods and beautiful buildings, yet with the Savior standing outside trying to get in.

We find in Luke the rich fool who said, "This will I do: I will pull down my barns, and build greater; and there will I bestow all my fruits and my goods. And I will say to my soul, Soul, thou hast much goods laid up for many years; take thine ease, eat, drink, and be merry. But God said unto him, Thou fool, this night thy soul shall be required of thee: then whose shall those things be, which thou hast provided?" (Luke 12:18-20). The whole Bible teaches that plenty, however justly it may be acquired, constitutes a great danger.

After the Methodist society became established and had circled the world and were growing in number, John Wesley admitted, "We are in a peculiar paradox in our Methodist societies." He said, "I have noticed that as soon as a group of people meet together and form a society and subscribe to the New Testament doctrines and bring their lives into line with the truth, they immediately get honest, frugal, saving, hardworking, and upright and industrious and the result is they lay out money."

Then he said, "As soon they get some money, they begin to trust it. As soon as they begin to trust their money, they cease to be holy and spiritual, frugal, hardworking, honest, good, and so they backslide and so, here is the vicious circle. Get right with God and you become frugal, saving, honest, hardworking, serious. That is the path to get rich. When you get rich, you tend to backslide." He said, "Here's the vicious circle. What are we going to do?"

Leave it to John Wesley. He was not going to be licked by a vicious circle. He said, "I have the answer." He said, "Be honest, holy, hardworking, frugal, saving, get all you can, then give it all away, and that way you'll never backslide. Make all you can, save all you can, give all you can."

That is exactly what John Wesley did. The wealth of England would have been laid at his feet—at least the common people would have laid their money there—but when he died, he died with 28 pounds, approximately $130, after a lifetime. He lived 83 years and died with $130. He did not have to make out a will. It took more than that to bury him.

Being accustomed to plenty is deadly if you do not know what to do with it. No boy gets so arrogant and reckless as a boy who is newly rich. No girl gets as extravagant and wild as the girl in the big city making good money. I do not say that it always happens, but the temptation is there.

Over the years, I have seen young men who, while they were in high school and college, struggled, fought, prayed, loved God and got along on a little. Then they met a girl who had the same experience fighting her way through and working after hours to get enough to continue and help with the home. She had a little, he had a little, and then they met each other and got married. Then they got out of school, settled down, got good jobs and used his sanctified Christian intelligence to get a good position.

Soon, the money was coming his way hand over fist, and they moved into a finer home, got a bigger car, a bigger television, and a finer model of everything. They began to come to choir less often and to prayer meeting rarely and to church less frequently; and they began to take long holiday excursions and then longer ones. Soon they backslid. Prosperity is dangerous for a Christian.

How to Handle Prosperity

What can you do? Am I saying that I wish all Christians were poor people? If all the people were poor, how would we ever manage to keep missionaries on the field? How would we ever promote Christian publishing societies? How would we ever get books out to the public? How would we ever keep schools going? How would we finance God's work to keep our missionaries going, our radio programs alive and our books flowing? How would we do it?

No, it is not God's will that His people should all be poor. It is God's will that His people should prosper but know what to do with prosperity. I give you three rules to handle prosperity well.

1. *Thank God reverently.* Never receive a raise, never receive anything but that you reverently thank God and acknowledge the source of it and know that it comes from the Father of Lights, from whence every good gift comes.

2. *Share it generously.* If you do not share generously, it will begin to canker and rust your spirit and soul. The bigger the bank account, the smaller the heart, unless you share it so generously that your conscience feels good about it and God is satisfied.

3. *Walk circumspectly.* If you have plenty, thank God reverently, share it generously and walk circumspectly: "And take heed to yourselves, lest at any time your hearts be overcharged with surfeiting, and drunken-

ness, and cares of this life, and so that day come upon you unawares" (Luke 21:34).

This verse is talking about prosperity. "Your hearts be overcharged with surfeiting" is overeating. "Drunkenness" is drinking. "The cares of this life" means that the poorer a man is, the fewer cares he has; and the more he gets, the more cares he has. If he allows his heart to be overcharged, overwhelmed with these earthly things, the day of Christ shall come upon him unawares. "For as a snare shall it come on all them that dwell on the face of the whole earth. Watch ye therefore, and pray always, that ye may be accounted worthy to escape all these things that shall come to pass, and to stand before the Son of man" (Luke 21:35-36).

The urgent exhortation is that we might watch carefully, lest prosperity with its surfeiting, its overeating, its careless drinking and the cares of this life make us unfit for that Day, and we should be caught like a little animal in a snare when our Lord comes. Rather, we ought to pray that we might be worthy to escape these things and stand before the Son of Man.

The Danger of Adversity

It is an odd thing, but not only is prosperity dangerous, but so is adversity dangerous. "Give me neither poverty nor riches; feed me with food convenient for me: Lest if I be full, and deny thee, and say, Who is the LORD? or lest I be poor, and steal, and take the name of my God in vain" (Prov. 30:8-9). That is a wise and practical little verse from the Old Testament. Adversity means financial reverses or physical afflictions.

Financial Adversity

Financial reversal is the exact opposite of prosperity, and yet it is dangerous too, especially if it follows prosperity. Some people are so habitually in a state of having no money or little money that it is called impecuniosity, and there is nothing to react from. If you have been reasonably prosperous and then you have a reverse, it is especially dangerous because prosperity tends to make us soft. We are soft compared with our fathers.

Dr. Samuel Johnson said, "Resolve not to be poor: whatever you have, spend less. Poverty is a great enemy to human happiness; it certainly destroys liberty, and it makes some virtues impracticable and others extremely difficult."

Too much poverty will beat you down, sicken you, weaken you and make you old before your time. If you have had prosperity and then you are plunged into reverses, you are likely to blow up because you have been made soft. Too much prosperity will make you soft.

To have prosperity suddenly removed from us means that it is likely to take away the rock of our trust and plunge us into panic.

Physical Adversity

It is an odd thing that people react to physical illness in two opposite ways. Some react by using it as a means of grace. David said, "Before I was afflicted I went astray: but now have I kept thy word" (Ps. 119:67). While David was ill, he had time to think it over and pray and wait on God, and he used his affliction as a means of grace. Others, as soon as they are touched with physical affliction, throw in the towel.

Some people know how to use physical affliction. David did: "Before I was afflicted, I went astray, I got careless. When I got sick, I had time to think it over and I got right with God." Now in any case, financial reversals or physical afflictions are dangers, but this little verse has comforted me: "If thou faint in the day of adversity, thy strength is small" (Prov. 24:10). It does not promise anything; it just makes a rather uncomplimentary statement about a man, and yet I get help out of that verse.

How to Avoid These Dangers

The danger of having too much, and the danger of suddenly having not enough; or the danger of wellness and then sudden physical adversity or death. Opposite ends related to each other. One is the seamy side of the other, but they are both dangerous. Against them we need a rock and a shelter, a hiding place and a fortress, a buckler and a shield and strength; we need help from the lions of prosperity and adversity. The fat lion is prosperity, and the scrawny, hungry lion is adversity; they are both lions, and they are both sources of danger. How do we avoid them? I offer four rules.

Get Thoroughly Detached from Earthly Possessions

If you are not detached from earthly possessions, every dollar you accumulate will be a blight on your spirit. If you have an understanding with God that goes clear down deep about who owns everything, then your increasing riches will not hurt you at all, because they are not yours. You will hold them for the Giver. God gave them, and you hold them for Him.

Blessed is the man who possesses nothing. If we possess nothing, God will allow us to have plenty. If we possess anything, we are cursed by it. So get it outside of you. Get thoroughly detached from earthly possessions. Look out for a thrill if you get a raise. Look out for a thrill if you get more money. Look out for a thrill that comes from possessions.

Break the Grip of the World's Philosophies

A true Christian has said goodbye to the philosophies of the world and keeping up with the Joneses. The world makes us ashamed to wear a suit if it is not the latest model; ashamed to drive a car that is not the latest; ashamed to live in a house that is not the latest grotesque monstrosity. It makes us ashamed to be a little behind the times. But a man who is big enough to know that he is above all times is big enough to dare to live boldly where he pleases—in style or out of style.

It is no act of righteousness to be out of style. It is no sin to be in style. The glory lies in giving not one care to either, but saying, "I'll live decently and respectably and strike a happy medium and go my way, and I don't care what the world says." The world feeds it into us from the time we are in kindergarten and makes us ashamed to wear clothing a little too long. Ashamed not to have a bicycle, or it has to be the best one. If we have a car, it has to be the best one. Whatever we have has to be the best.

If you do not get free from prosperity and adversity, it will grind you to pieces. Prosperity, if you have it, will kill you; and adversity, if you have it, will grind you. If you will get free from the world's philosophies and dare to be a Christian, standing on your own feet, thanking God for what you have and being an independent Christian, neither one of them will harm you. God will take you out from between the lower and the upper millstone.

Jesus never wore a garment somebody did not make for Him. Jesus never owned anything that would have sold at auction, probably, for more than a dollar and a half; and yet Jesus was the Lord of glory, and the riches of the world were His. He could have spoken to the stones and they would have been gold. He could have spoken to the trees and they would have turned to rich wheat bread. He could have spoken to the very air and it would have blown riches to Him; but He walked calmly, quietly through the world and left one garment behind Him.

If God gave you possessions, thank God for them. But break with the grip of the world's philosophies and make God everything. If God is everything to you, you can have anything else and it will not hurt you. If God is little or nothing to you, anything will hurt you.

Accept Your Status as a Pilgrim

You are a pilgrim, not a resident, here on earth. You are passing through. You are a Christian. We build no nest here for our hearts. In the spring, you will see a brown bird with spotted breast and a white ring around its perfectly round eyes, and it will be down on the ground among the bushes, scratching about, all by itself. It will be singing the gentlest, softest little song you ever heard in all your life. That is an ovenbird—a migratory bird.

The flight song of the ovenbird is one of the great things to hear on the North American continent, but there are no ovenbirds in Chicago. The ones that come here are migratory. They are passing through from where they were to where they are going to go, and they just stop around long enough to give you a little taste of what their beautiful song is. They are shy, and you cannot get near them, but if you are real patient, you will hear them sing; ovenbirds are on their way from the South to the North to hatch, to raise their little brood. Next fall, they will be back to scratch under your window again. They are migrating.

God's children are not resident birds, but are migratory birds, passing through from where they were to where they are going. Where they are going, of course, is God Almighty's heaven. We are migratory birds; we are pilgrims passing through. This is not our home; so while we have things, let us use them reverently, thankfully and wisely. Let us give them generously as we get shed from the love of things and people's opinions and ourselves and our money and our clothing and our possessions.

We are pilgrims, and He who guides through the boundless air the certain flight of the bird will also guide us until we arrive at last on those shores that are washed by the water that flows from the throne of God. It is well worth waiting for, brethren.

Higher Ground
Johnson Oatman, Jr. (1856–1926)

I'm pressing on the upward way,
New heights I'm gaining every day;
Still praying as I onward bound,
"Lord, plant my feet on higher ground."

I want to live above the world,
Though Satan's darts at me are hurled;
For faith has caught the joyful sound,
The song of saints on higher ground.

I want to scale the utmost height
And catch a gleam of glory bright;
But still I'll pray till rest I've found,
"Lord, lead me on to higher ground."

Lord, lift me up, and let me stand
By faith on Canaan's tableland;
A higher plane than I have found,
Lord, plant my feet on higher ground.

My heart has no desire to stay
Where doubts arise and fears dismay;
Though some may dwell where these abound,
My prayer, my aim, is higher ground.

12

THE DANGER OF POSTPONED LIVING

And as he reasoned of righteousness, temperance, and judgment to come, Felix trembled, and answered, Go thy way for this time; when I have a convenient season, I will call for thee.

ACTS 24:25

If Jesus Christ cannot make a man good on earth, then He cannot justify him in heaven. If Jesus Christ cannot deliver me from the power of sin in this life, I do not believe He can deliver me before the face of my Father in heaven. But as a regenerated, justified and delivered man, I believe He can do both. I believe that He justifies before the Father those who believe in Him, and He also delivers from sin those who repent of their sins and believe in Him.

We have righteousness, temperance and judgment yet to come, and we have belief on Jesus Christ for moral change in this life. Not everybody responds to the fact that Jesus has something for the saved man and woman to do. Some ignore it or reject it, while others surrender and accept the good life in Jesus Christ. Some join the Church and go to work, witness and seek to grow in the grace and knowledge of the Lord

Jesus Christ. Some simply acknowledge that salvation is good and that they want to hear more about it, but they postpone it indefinitely.

Remember, you have not done anything about truth until you have acted on it. If it is a statement, it is to be believed. If it is a command, it is to be obeyed. If you have not believed or obeyed, you have not done anything, and you have postponed your Christian life.

I'll Do It Tomorrow

It permeates our lives. It follows us everywhere we go. That great beast says, "Not now, do this tomorrow. Tomorrow I will do it, and it shall be so." So the urgings of the Holy Spirit get postponed. They are not denied or rejected, but simply postponed for some more convenient time. Tomorrow and tomorrow, all shall be well. If the Word of God is not obeyed, it is rejected just as surely as it would be by a seminary that denied that the Bible is true.

There are two kinds of unbelief. There is the outspoken unbelief, and there is the unbelief that is too cowardly to say, but the person never obeys, and therefore proves to be as bad a case of unbelief as the other. If I believe, I will do something about it. If somebody tells me there is a bomb in the room, and I believe it, I will get out of the room. If I do not believe it, I will stay. It depends upon whether I believe it or not. If I yell in the night, "Fire, get out of your house," and you, my neighbor, do not believe what I am saying, you will turn over in bed and say, "That drunk man's out there again."

It all depends upon whether you believe a thing or not. If you haven't done anything about your salvation yet, then you don't believe it in a "saving" way. Let me take this out of the realm of theory and doctrine and show you what I mean.

The Tragedy of the Postponed Spiritual Life

We are forever thinking about something to do, but we say, "Tomorrow, I will do it." You bought a book and you intended to read it, but you have not got around to reading it yet. It is right there on the shelf, right where you put it. You tell yourself, "I'm going to read that book when I come home." Then you come home in the evening and you want to know how the world and the government are getting along, so you watch the news and the commentators hash over the news.

Then supper's ready and you eat, and afterward there is an interesting program on television, and you watch it. Then another one comes along, and you stretch and yawn and say, "I've had a hard day." So you go to bed without reading the book. You decide, "Next summer I'll read that book, when I have more time."

Next summer comes, and you go on a long trip or vacation and take the book along, and still you do not have time to read the book. Let's say the book on the shelf is God's Word. God has a book based upon the big, grand story of His plan to save people, and it has helped thousands but has never gotten inside of you. You are simply postponing dealing with God's truth.

As Christians, we say, "Tomorrow I'm going to catch up on that. I am going to read that Book. I am going to start the habit of being faithful in church. I know I should be a daily Bible reader, and tomorrow I'm going to start that."

You listen to a good sermon and say to yourself, *I need to get back to reading my Bible. I have to begin. I'm going to do it.* But you do not do it. A little slack here, a little slack there, or you read a book of daily devotions predigested for you by somebody else, and that is your Bible for the day. You say, "Oh, this is only temporary. I'm going to get to it soon."

It has been years now, and still you have not read through your Bible, and if you have, you have not read through it twice. Everybody, by the time he has been a Christian for five years, should have read the Bible through more than once and should have read parts of it through with loving care. You meant to do it, but you have not.

Do Not Postpone Daily Private Prayer

You may say, "I'm going to pray. As it is now, I just pray when I'm scared, and before meals, and I mumble something before I go to bed. But I am going to start to really pray. I'm going to take time out and really do it."

If you do not learn to pray every day by yourself, you will never get far in the kingdom of God. If you say, "But I have family prayer," that is not enough. If you say, "I pray in church on Sunday," that is not enough. Jesus said, "When thou prayest, enter into thy closet, and when thou hast shut thy door, pray to thy Father which is in secret" (Matt. 6:6). If you have not been doing that, it may be one reason your Christian life is so weak. We have to learn the habit of daily prayer.

One man prayed five times a day, "Evening, and morning, and at noon, will I pray, and cry aloud: and he shall hear my voice" (Ps. 55:17). I am not setting times for you, but you will have to have a place to pray where nobody hears you. When people hear us, we tend to edit our prayers to suit the company we are in.

The Greeks used to say that if there is ever a time a man is honest, it is when he appears before the gods. How much more is this true of a Christian. If there is ever a time when we need to be honest, it is when we are alone in the presence of God. If you do not learn to pray every day—and for some people it is a lot, and for some people it is a little—it is going to be a rather ragged life. There will be a little bit of fruit. But if you want to drink deep of the fountains of God, you are going to have to spend some time in prayer, and you cannot put that off until tomorrow or the next day or the next day; you're going to have to start now.

Do Not Postpone Gathering for Prayer

Many good Christians never show up to prayer meetings. Announce a banquet and everybody will be there. Announce a prayer meeting and only a few will show up. You can tell the power of a church by the number of people who attend the prayer meeting, no question about it.

"I know I should go, and I'm going to go next week." Next week comes around and you do not show up. If you were as faithful in going to work as you are going to prayer meeting, you probably would not have a job for long. Nothing keeps us away from work, but almost anything will keep us away from prayer meeting for the simple reason that we are looking for a dodge, a place to hide.

We say, "I'll start next week." If everybody who intended to go to prayer meeting went to prayer meeting, we would not have room for them all. We say, "Next week," but we do not do it. And so that beast eats up your tomorrows, and you fall victim to postponement.

Do Not Postpone Giving Back What Belongs to God

If you say, "I've been careless with my money, but then I've had to put my children through school, and besides that, things haven't gone so good. I'm going to start tithing, and then in addition to that, I'm going to start giving extra. And I'm going to do that next year." Next year comes, but you do not do it. If you remember, you have been saying the same thing for a long time. The taxes are high. Remember the time when everybody thought it was a terrible thing for the Lord to demand the tenth, then the government takes 30 percent and nobody dares say a word about it.

We say, "I'm going to start giving," then some pseudo-crisis comes up. Junior has to have braces on his teeth. The wife's arches have fallen and she has to have special shoes. And so it finally turns out that the Lord does not get anything. At the judgment seat of Christ, we are all going to have to tell Him why we postponed what we knew we should be doing.

Do Not Postpone Speaking to the Lost

Then we say, "I'm going to speak to that lost brother-in-law of mine; I'm going to speak to him. I'm going to talk to people about the Lord. I really am." But we do not. We go to see them, and we eat and talk and listen to music, but we do not talk to them about the Lord. Each day we live in anticipation of the next, and we say, "Tomorrow, I'll go see that friend." Then we do not do it, and so our service is not yet done and the kingdom of God suffers; the lost remain unsaved and we have not obeyed.

What about the Christian who desires victory in his life? Oh, how many of God's people want victory! Announce a sermon on the victorious life and immediately the church will be filled. Everybody wants victory; everybody wants power; everybody wants the deeper life; but we say tomorrow . . . tomorrow. Tomorrow comes and goes, and we say, "Next week, for sure."

If you want to be holy—if you want to serve God—you have to give time to God. Grace and holiness take time, and the cultivation of the Spirit takes time. Do you want to be holy? Do you want a deep faith? Then you have to give God time, and not just intend to. You say, "I believe you, brother. I'm going to do it." But you never do.

Perhaps you are someone who will never get victory until you write a letter to somebody with whom you had a fuss. It is something that needs to be done, and I have seen that kind of reconciliatory act work wonders. Yet some say, "I'll write that letter tomorrow."

"Tomorrow I'll establish family prayer." Or, "I'll establish family prayer when I get my new work hours." The new hours come and go, and you do not have family prayer. You mumble some kind of grace at the dinner table.

"I'll be reconciled to that enemy. I'll do that act of kindness." The world is a mean, sinful world. We are here to do kind things for people, and I recommend you start doing them, because you will not be around for the next generation.

David served his generation by the will of God before he fell asleep (died). No man has any right to fall asleep until he has served his generation. You cannot serve the generation that is past, and you cannot, except indirectly, serve the generation to come. But you can serve the present generation.

Do Not Postpone Kindness and Serving Your Family

A little boy asked his father to help him build a little hut in the backyard, but his father was always tired and said, "No, not tonight."

The next night, when the dad came home, the little boy said, "Daddy, will you help me build the hut tonight?"

The father said, "I'll do it, son, one of these days. I'll do it." But he never did.

Then one day he came home and the boy said, "Daddy, will you help me build my hut tonight?"

"Son, I am awfully tired. If you will put it off until tomorrow night, I'll even buy new lumber and I'll help you build your hut." So the little fellow went off to bed with his face shining. He was finally going to have his hut built out of new lumber.

About ten o'clock the next morning, this businessman father got a call. "Come to the hospital, your boy's been hurt. On his way to school he was hit by a truck."

The father got there and found the little crushed form of his son. The son recognized his father, but he could not talk much. The father put his ear down and heard, "Well, Daddy, we didn't get our hut built, did we?"

The man said, "Oh, God, if I could have him back just one day. If I could have him back just one evening, no matter how tired I am, I would help him build that hut. I kept putting it off and putting it off." All he will have for the rest of his life is the memory of a kind deed postponed.

There are people waiting for that kind deed, maybe not insistently asking for it, but they are waiting for it. You meant to lend your good heart, but you have not done it. You are falling into the trap of postponed living.

To the backslider the Lord is saying, "Come home." You are postponing your return to the Lord; but remember what the prodigal son said? "I will arise and go!" He did not say, "Tomorrow, I will arise and go." He said, "I will arise and go now." So, he arose and went. There is only one way to make good on an intention, and that is to turn it into action.

Do Not Postpone Answering God's Call

When the Lord comes beside the lost soul and offers forgiveness, cleansing, deliverance and light, and the lost soul says, "Go thy way, some other time, some more convenient season. Tomorrow, I will stop that evil life. Tomorrow, I will turn from the wicked thing that I'm doing that I know grieves God." But he does not.

"Tomorrow I'll confess," but he does not. "Tomorrow, I'll make a public confession of Christ before the church. I will go to the front and become a Christian. Tomorrow, next week." But he does not do it.

That is the history of how many tens of thousands of "I will be saved tomorrow" souls perish today. To me this is an awful thing. I believe God put the stories in the Bible as markers for us. They are white crosses erected at the crossroads of life, saying "Look out here, because here's where men perish."

I believe that the story of Felix in Acts 24 is one such marker on the highway of life, saying to all of us, "Look out, right at this point is a hairpin turn." Felix perished at the hairpin turn; he postponed living. Felix lost that which he could not afford to lose.

If Felix had lost his job, he could afford that. He did lose it anyway, two years later. If he lost his wife, Priscilla, he could have afforded that. If he had lost his health, he could have afforded that. If he had lost his life itself, he could have afforded that. We all have to die. But he lost that which no man can afford to lose. *Felix lost his soul.* No man can afford to lose his soul. No one can afford to lose that precious treasure to which we say, "Tomorrow . . . tomorrow . . . tomorrow."

What are you going to do? Are you going to live today, or are you going to postpone living until tomorrow, and never live? Are you going to get right with God today, or are you going to postpone it and never get right? Are you going to seek the Holy Spirit for Himself, and be filled with the Spirit now? Or do you want to postpone and never be filled with the Spirit? Are you going to seek to be victorious in your Christian life, or are you going to say, "Tomorrow or next week, I'll talk to my pastor about it." If you postpone it, maybe you will never get to it.

Softly and Tenderly
Will L. Thompson (1847–1909)

Softly and tenderly Jesus is calling,
Calling for you and for me.
See, on the portals,
He's waiting and watching,
Watching for you and for me.

Why should we tarry
When Jesus is pleading,
Pleading for you and for me?
Why should we linger
And heed not His mercies,
Mercies for you and for me?

Time is now fleeting;
The moments are passing,
Passing from you and from me.
Shadows are gathering;
Death's night is coming,
Coming for you and for me.

Oh for the wonderful
Love He has promised,
Promised for you and for me!
Though we have sinned,
He has mercy and pardon,
Pardon for you and for me.

Come home, come home.
Ye who are weary, come home.
Earnestly, tenderly Jesus is calling,
Calling, "O sinner, come home!"

PART III

. . . .

THE PATH
TO OVERCOMING
THESE
CHALLENGES

13

RESISTING THE WORLD'S PROPAGANDA

Therefore let us not sleep, as do others; but let us watch and be sober.

1 THESSALONIANS 5:6

But the end of all things is at hand: be ye therefore sober,
and watch unto prayer.

1 PETER 4:7

The curse of spiritual lethargy in the evangelical church has created a vulnerability to the insidious attacks of the enemy. In order to overcome the world and its influences, we must understand the dynamics of those attacks and the booby traps placed by our enemy, the devil. For one, I recommend that we carefully watch lest we fall into the snare of propagandism—the battle for our minds.

Our enemy believes in slavery. There are two kinds of slavery. There is the slavery of the body, which seeks to control conduct by physical force. That slavery was once in the United States, much to our everlasting historical shame. But there is another kind of slavery that seems to me to be so much worse. It is the slavery of the mind that is achieved by means of insidious ideas that are supplied to the mind. Once these ideas get our focus, our obedience is rendered willingly and we are un-aware that we have become slaves to the enemy's propaganda. In fact, we are quite satisfied and have no desire to be free from the snare of this propaganda.

Put chains on a man's ankles and wrists, and he knows it. Look deep into his eyes and you will find there the sullen revolt of the free human spirit against the bonds of slavery. But con-ditioning the mind creates a slave who doesn't know it. We are constantly being fed harmful ideas that we adopt and learn to believe in, thinking they are all right, and so we ignorantly fol-low. This is done without our knowing that a keen, sharp, un-scrupulous mind is seeking to control us.

The Battle Is On!

The greatest war ever fought is not in the history books. Those wars were wars of body against body, gun against gun, sword against sword, and battalion against battalion. The greatest war is still being waged today by every effective technique cre-ated to get us to stop thinking for ourselves. It is being waged by the media, in all its various forms, from hard news reporting to "entertainment." If you could suddenly stand off objectively and look at your mind and see how much the media has fed into it and how you have come to be more or less a creature in-fluenced by the media, you would be shocked and spend days in fasting and prayer to get free from it.

Another technique is that of the school system. We must have our schools, of course, but our education system is feed-ing the minds of our young people in such a way as to control their thinking. Then there is the effective dissemination of ideas from radio, television, film, magazines, books and the In-ternet. Whoever controls this media is controlling the ideas and the thinking of the American people today.

One of the most successful techniques ever devised by the mind of man for the control of mass thinking is advertising. Advertisers are the best educators in the world, and by expensive and carefully thought-out means, they are busy controlling our thinking. The object is to get everyone to think the same on certain subjects, such as life, love, money, pleasure, marriage, values, religion, the future, God, our relation to God, and all the rest. They are eager for everyone to think the same about everything.

We Are All Philosophers

While only some people get the reputation for being philosophers, every person is a philosopher. The kid who carries a switchblade or gun and attacks another innocent kid on the street and kills him or cuts him up is a philosopher too. If you press him and push him into a corner, he will come through with reasons why he did what he did. And reasons are philosophy.

Wherever you have reason for doing some action, it makes you a philosopher. Therefore, everybody is a philosopher. We all have a certain philosophy of life. We look out upon life and see it from a certain viewpoint. Whether we write great books and call ourselves by that name, or whether we are simple people who would smile at the thought that we are philosophers, we are all philosophers, nonetheless.

Who is going to control your philosophy? Who is going to determine your outlook on life? Who is going to decide? You say, "I do that myself." Do not make me laugh. You do not do that yourself at all; you only think you do.

Then there is our philosophy on love. What is this love business anyhow? All you have to do is press a button and you will be told what it is and what it is not. We get our ideas about human love between the sexes, and love in society, from TV, film, magazines and all kinds of advertising.

When it comes to a philosophy of money, we believe what the press tells us to think of money, or we believe what we have learned at school. When it comes to our attitude toward pleasures—innocent or harmful—we learn from the world. The world uses effective techniques to get us to think the way it wants us to think—especially about God, religion, our values and the future.

What I think about money is important, but what I think about God is most important. There has not been a time since the Great Awakening, under Jonathan Edwards, when there was more religion in the country, more persons trying to persuade us to think a certain way about religion and God and human values, the future life and our relation to God in the future life.

Resist the Counsel of the Ungodly

We are going to be what they make of us unless, of course, we stage a revolt, which I trust I may stir up. The strategy is to control our conduct by disseminating ideas and to gain acceptance for the counsel of the ungodly. The Bible talks about the counsel of the ungodly and pronounces a blessing upon the man who walks not in it. We always must keep in mind that this is a fallen world, and whatever originates in the world is bound to be bad and godless. Whatever originates in organized society, with thoughts from fallen minds and fallen hearts, is godless.

The Word of God was given to counteract godless counsel among godly men and to form our minds, not by all the techniques of the media, but by God Himself. The God who made us gave us a Bible—His Word—and sent the Holy Spirit to interpret it to us in order that He may control our minds; that

He who is the source of all blessing and love, and who made our minds, might mold them again and remake them. That God wants to control our minds, and He has no hesitation in saying that we are to have the mind of Christ.

Somebody is going to control your mind. Who is it going to be? Is it going to be the advertiser? Is it going to be the public school? Is it going to be the media? Or is it going to be God? You have to make up your mind on that, my friend. Whether you want to or not, somebody is going to control your mind; who is it going to be? "Wherewithal shall a young man cleanse his way? by taking heed thereto according to thy word" (Ps. 119:9).

Seek the Counsel of God

How shall my ignorance become wisdom? Through the counsel of the Word of God. How shall my false notions become right notions? By being corrected by the Word of God. How shall my darkness become light? By this Book that is a light unto my pathway. It is from this Book, interpreted by the Holy Spirit, that I gain the right ideas about love and marriage and life and money and pleasures and values, and God and my relation to God, and the future life and my status in that life.

The warfare is between the counsel of the ungodly and the counsel of God. Which shall control your mind? You are a pawn and a puppet caught in between, and if you are not awakened to it, you will learn the ways of Babylon and Egypt. You will pick up their notions and think the way they think and value what they value and love what they love and ignore what they ignore.

Slaves to Jesus Christ

The Christian receives another mind. It is the redeemed mind, a re-created mind committed to Christ. You say, "Is not that another kind of slavery?" Yes. It is the slavery of love. It is the slavery of worship. It is the slavery of extreme joy. It is the slavery of the highest ecstasy.

The apostle Paul, who lived in a state where slaves were a common sight on the street, said, "I am a slave of Jesus Christ" (see Rom. 1:1). Wherever the word "servant" occurs in the New Testament, you can write "slave," for that is what Paul meant. He had no thought of a paid servant who comes at nine, leaves at five and gets his pay and goes home. That is unknown in the Bible. Paul openly told the people, at every opportunity, that he was a slave to God Almighty and to Jesus Christ.

But there is the freedom. Love never feels slavery, and love never knows bondage. That obedience to Jesus Christ, which Paul called slavery, is not the slavery that imposes itself from the outside by laws, nor by the introduction of alien ideas into the mind. It is the happy, joyous bondage of freedom and love; and the holiest and most free creature in heaven above is the angel that is nearest the throne of God.

Those creatures that bow and spread their wings, and run swift to do the will of God, and have no mind but God and no will but His, are the most free creatures in the entire universe. Those creatures—that's us—who try to be free from the will of God succeed only in becoming victims to the propagandists who want to make us think the same as they think and feel the same as they feel about things; they are slaves.

The bird that flies in the air is free, and yet the laws of aerodynamics bind it. The stars that move in and around their ancient and unmeasured orbits are free, because they are doing the will of God. Wherever we do the will of God, we are free. Wherever we break from the will of God, we are slaves. It says in the book of Romans that he who sins is a slave of sin, and he who does the will of God is the free servant of God (see Rom. 6:16).

Wake from Spiritual Lethargy

Suppose there was a law passed in Washington, D.C., that said you cannot go to church, and if you do, you will be fined. And if you repeat the offense, you will be jailed. We would know where we stood, and we would stand up and put our chins high and say, "If God helps me, I'll never come under that decree. I'll go to church when I please, and I'll pray to God as I want. My fathers founded this nation dedicated to the proposition that every man should worship God according to the dictates of his own heart."

However, that is not what is happening. The devil is too much of a strategist to treat us like that. He is busy brainwashing us and conditioning us, little by little, and feeding his ideas into the Church. As the ideas of the ungodly enter the Church, the counsel of God goes out. My crusade is to wake the Church from its spiritual lethargy, rousing it to the fact that it is being brainwashed and propagandized into accepting that which it would never accept if it were a law in Washington.

We have an example in Lot and his family, back in Sodom. He went there for economic reasons, because the grass was green. He rapidly rose to be an important member of the city; he sat in the gate. His family was quite well known in the city and they were slowly propagandized; they were brainwashed.

Lot resisted it. He had had enough contact with Abraham—he had sat where Abraham sat and walked with Abraham. He had heard Abraham pray, and after having heard Abraham offer prayers to God, he never could quite accept the brainwashing of Sodom. Lot "vexed his righteous soul" (2 Pet. 2:8).

Thank God for those words "vexed" and "righteous" in the same man's heart. He vexed his righteous soul. He was a part of Sodom, but he hated it. When Sodom put on her big shows, he heard in his memory the voice of Abraham rise in prayer. It still rang in his ears, and it poisoned all of the pleasures of Sodom. But he was not big enough to get up and walk out. For economic reasons, he stayed in Sodom, hating it.

But Lot's family was not so strong. They were poisoned and propagandized into becoming Sodomites. When God Almighty raised His mighty judgment on Sodom and sent fire out from His fingertips to destroy that city, Lot fled with his two daughters; his wife never quite made it. She had been brainwashed, and she looked back at the city. She came under the same judgment as the city. Lot escaped with his two daughters, but even his two daughters had been poisoned.

When Israel went down into Egypt for 400 years, they were subjected to the propaganda of Egypt, even as they kept themselves aloof. They learned the ways of Egypt and came out idolaters. They were idolaters until Moses brought down the law from Mount Sinai, corrected their wrong thinking, put away their idolatry, laid the law down for them and gave them the Word of God.

Slowly, the nations got among them over in Palestine after they had entered the Promised Land. They learned the ways of the heathen, Jebusites, the Hittites and all the rest of them that should have been purged out of the land. The Israelites slowly learned the evil ways of the nations. You know the result was a Babylonian captivity that finally destroyed idolatry. Israel has never worshiped idols since she spent 70 years in captivity in Babylon.

Stand Clear from the World

What is it going to take to wake up the Church . . . to keep the world from using the Church to achieve its own ends? I wonder what kind of Babylon and beside what waters we are going to sit bitterly and hang our harps and refuse to sing? I wonder what Ezra and Nehemiah will be sent to lead us back to the land again, purged of our idolatry and washed this time by the blood of the Lamb?

The only way to help the world is to stay free from its brainwashing. The man who has adopted its ways can never help it. It is by standing aloof from its ways that we can help it. The aloof man is the only man that can do any good. You can only help a sinner by going contrary to him.

There is only one way to bless mankind, and that is by opposing mankind. For wherever mankind is wrong, and wherever he is different from God, it means that brother must be divided from brother and husband from wife and children from parents. Jesus said, "If any man come to me, and hate not his father, and mother, and wife, and children, and brethren, and sisters, yea, and his own life also, he cannot be my disciple" (Luke 14:26). You must be sober and prayerfully beware the world's propagandas. Do not sell yourself, and do not allow yourself to be slowly reasoned into wrong by the counsel of the ungodly. Better to be a radical on the right side than weak on the wrong side. Better go too far than not far enough.

When the world says, "Oh, you're narrow," you say, "Maybe I am narrow, but the way is narrow, and the path to heaven isn't as broad as a 16-lane highway. You know why I am too narrow? I'm walking with my God."

Maybe our Pilgrim Fathers were too narrow. I rather think they were when they told the children they could not laugh on the Sabbath Day. I think they went too far when they said a man could not kiss his wife on the Sabbath. I think they went too far when they said you could not walk down the lane in your garden, pick up an onion and eat it or any fruit; you could not stand there idly and look at the sun and say that's harvesting. I think they went too far, but better to have a strong testimony in the right direction, even if it goes too far, than to have all this weak compromise that is cursing us today.

Let us stand out, even if it is extreme in the eyes of the world. Let us be known as Christians separated unto God; and if the world laughs and the other churches laugh and say, "What's the matter with you Christians? Are you holy rollers?" Say, "No, I'm not as holy as I want to be. I'm just a believer in the Word of God; and if I go too far, you'll forgive me, but I'd rather go too far than not far enough."

The only slavery I recommend is the sweet slavery of Jesus' yoke, which is easy, and His burden is light (see Matt. 11:30). The yoke of Jesus is a love yoke—the yoke that binds us to the essence and center and sum of all that is desirable and loving and wonderful and good. When you put His yoke upon you, the yoke of the world will drop away.

Beneath the Cross of Jesus
Elizabeth C. Clephane (1830–1869)

Beneath the cross of Jesus
I fain would take my stand,
the shadow of a mighty rock
within a weary land;
a home within the wilderness,
a rest upon the way,
from the burning of the noontide heat,
and the burden of the day.

Upon that cross of Jesus
mine eye at times can see
the very dying form of One
who suffered there for me;

and from my stricken heart with tears
two wonders I confess:
the wonders of redeeming love
and my unworthiness.

I take, O cross, thy shadow
for my abiding place;
I ask no other sunshine than
the sunshine of his face;
content to let the world go by,
to know no gain nor loss,
my sinful self my only shame,
my glory all the cross.

14

CONTEMPLATING
OUR WAYS

*Come now, and let us reason together, saith the LORD: though your sins
be as scarlet, they shall be as white as snow; though they be red like
crimson, they shall be as wool. If ye be willing and obedient, ye shall
eat the good of the land: but if ye refuse and rebel, ye shall be devoured
with the sword: for the mouth of the LORD hath spoken it.*

ISAIAH 1:18

The difference between a man and an animal is that a man reflects and a beast does not. The man and the animal start out with about the same amount of data. When a new puppy or a new calf is born into the world, it has about the same data furnished to the senses: the sun is there or it is not there. It is a warm day or it is a cold day. Things are comfortable or they are not comfortable. The mother is near or she is not.

The Bible does not hesitate to say that man and beasts are much alike. But it also says there is a gulf fixed between them, a difference that is so vast that it can never be explained. The chief difference will begin to manifest itself early, for the man reflects, and the beast does not. A child of three years old is already a walking question mark. The child reflects. But the calf born on the range or in the barn lives by its instincts and can grow to be old and die of old age, if permitted to, and still be living by its instincts. It will have learned little, and what it does learn will be low-grade and require practically no cogitation.

Not long after birth, the child begins to ask questions, but the animal never does.

There is a difference as vast as the difference that separates heaven from hell and the earth from the stars. It is the ability to consider our ways. Even though we, at some time in our life, do reflect on things, it is a tragic fact that after a while most people do not reflect on their ways. They may reflect, but they do not reflect on their own way. I wish I could get the adult males in this country to give as much consideration to their own souls as they give to the standings of their particular sports teams.

How would our country change if we could get people to spend four hours considering their own souls and their lives and their future with the concentrated attention they consider the strikeouts, the stolen bases and the rest of the baseball game?

A three-year-old says, "Mother, where did I come from?"

The mother replies, "You came from God."

"How did I get here?"

"Well, Jesus sent you."

"Is there a God, Mother, and can God see me? If I am in a room with no doors or windows, can He see me?"

Those are important basic questions that a grown man has long left behind. Who is going to win the national pennant is not an important basic question. But did you ever stop to think that the ball a pitcher throws has been made for him with such great precision as to allow him to throw the way he does? Did you ever stop to think he may have neglected his soul, neglected God and neglected heaven to get skill enough to throw that thing in a strike zone at least three times? Did you ever stop to think the rules are arbitrary and whimsical?

You could say a man is out on four strikes just as easy as three. And where is there any law in the universe that says three strikes and you're out? Furthermore, what difference does it make what happens to that ball? When a little artificial sphe-roid flies through space at 90 to 100 miles per hour, and some-body hits it, and 35,000 people are screaming themselves hoarse about that, what is the difference where it goes? It could fall down a gopher hole; it could get lost under a board or plank somewhere; it could go over onto the street and fall into the sewer; or a major league ballplayer could catch it.

What is the difference? "He got him out," you say. But what does that signify? That arbitrary expression does not have any root in nature anywhere. So goes most of man's activ-ity. This magnificent intellect that God has given man, this brilliant thing that can flash out like silver streams of light and reach back and take hold of history and pull it up so he can reach out in the future and pull it back; this intellect that can examine stars, moons, satellites and the depths of the earth and the deeps of the sea . . . how long since you have used what God has given you?

Think now of this imagination, this ability to consider, that we have. God says, "Consider your ways." "Come now, let us reason together." God is calling us to this. He is saying this to men who will not be here long. What are a few years against the solemn space we call eternity? What does it amount to? What is the difference?

Back in the days of Caesar, a man might die at 20 or 30; or he might die at 90. They were separated by a spread of 70 years; yet does it really matter now who died at 20 and who died at 90? What is the significance of 20 years set against 5,000 years, or set against eternity?

Against the backdrop of eternity, God tells us to consider. Here, I have given you something to consider. It makes no dif-ference who won that baseball game; it makes no difference whether he sunk that putt or not. Think on something eternal.

Think about something that matters. Give a little time to something that matters.

What God Asks of Your Soul

I believe there is a great God of justice and wisdom and logic and common sense in the heavens giving man such an amazing power to reflect. I believe God expects man to reflect; and if he will not do it, and if he will spend hours and hours, day after day, week after week, thinking about things that do not matter, and neglect the one thing that does, I see no place where God is under any obligation to take that man to heaven.

God put the door there and does not hide it, and the very stars in their courses tell where it is. God put the door there leading into the Kingdom. God calls, waits, stretches His hand out and says, "Come, come, come." He calls, invites, exhorts, urges us in a thousand ways and keeps it up for a lifetime. Yet if a man chooses to ignore that call and refuses to see that door, by what moral logic is God required to pick the man up by the scruff of his neck and take him to heaven when he spends a lifetime fooling with things that don't matter and refuses to consider the one thing that does?

A man commits a deep wrong against his own soul when he listens to a sermon and judges whether it was as good as the one he heard last week. What a terrible thought that with the final judgment coming, and our lives ebbing away, that we should compare instead of doing something about it. It is a deep wrong we do our own souls to vegetate like irrational creatures or spend our God-given faculties that were made to engage not stars and planets, but angels and seraphim, and God Himself. I say we do a terrible wrong against our own souls when we use such faculties as we have to fool, play and neglect our souls. James asks, what is your life? You possess the most precious thing in the world.

I was out in the country the other day and saw a hundred Hereford steers being fattened for the market. These were great, fine-looking fellows. I would guess they weighed 650 pounds each. They had everything, apparently, but they lacked one thing: they lacked that which the poorest man or woman has—a soul.

The skid-row bum that lies tonight in a stupor in some inner-city street has what the finest-blooded steer does not have. He has a soul; he has a life given to him from God. He has that which will have no termination but will go on and on and on. What is your life?

You possess it, and it is the most precious thing in the entire world, for it gives meaning to everything else. It is on loan from God to you. I do not know how God makes souls, but I know God lends them to us. When the new baby squalls his protest to the world, and his mother cuddles him warm against her breast, God says to that little one, when he can understand it, "Come now, and let us reason together. . . . Though your sins be as scarlet, they shall be as white as snow" (Isa. 17:18).

Though I were to suffer the pains of the damned for a thousand years, I would not give up that which I know to be my soul. My soul—that in me which is most like God of anything in the universe—I would not give it up. I would still say that a man is lucky to have a soul. What potentialities, what unbounded possibilities God has given to the man with a soul.

Young people do not know they have anything but glands; they live on their glands, they run on their glands. Yes, you have a set of glands, all right, and God gave them to you, and you ought not to be ashamed of them. But in addition to having glands, you have a soul. Think how many millions in this great land of ours do not know they have anything but glands.

They live by their glands and their nerves. Whoever can stir the glands of the greatest number of people can make millions of dollars a year. Running on glands turns us into feeble-minded, over-sexed, disappointed people who have forgotten they have a brain in their heads.

What Will You Do with What God Has Given You?

This life that God has given you, this soul, is what you make of it. Come and consider, think a little bit about it, consider your ways. God will not accept the responsibility for making it any more than what it is now, because God gave it to you with potentiality.

If I were to take 20 pounds of fine clay to a potter and commission him to make me a vase, I would not be responsible for anything but the plan. I would tell him I wanted the vase to be so high and so large. I want it to be decorated this way; I want it to be painted, and varnished, burnt, painted, varnished and burnt again.

I could give him the instructions for what I wanted, but if I came back and found a cheap pot all askew, lumpy and hopeless, I would not be responsible, because I had furnished the finest clay, laid the plan, given the commission; the potter who could not come through deserves no pay.

God has put in your hands that which is finer than the finest clay; God has given you a soul. Think what men have done with their souls. Bernard of Clairvaux wrote:

> Jesus, the very thought of Thee
> With sweetness fills my breast,
> But sweeter far Thy face to see,
> And in Thy presence rest.

The soul that God put in Bernard of Clairvaux is no finer than the soul He put in you or me or the most hardened criminal. God is not responsible if, with this life and intelligence and the Word of God before us, and the pleading of the Holy Spirit, we do nothing about it. You cannot blame heredity. You cannot blame environment. Scripture says, two shall be sleeping in one bed, two shall be plowing in, maybe they are brothers, or sisters, who slept together from the time they were born. Maybe they are two brothers or a father and son plowing in the field; one shall be taken and the other left (see Matt. 24:40-41). What happens to your soul cannot be blamed on heredity or on environment.

If you blame it on your parents and the way you were treated at home, I have no sympathy or message for you. "I had to go to school and I didn't have good clothes, and so I felt ashamed and I got an inferiority complex. My parents were religious and they took me to church and made me go to Sunday School, and I had holes in my shoes, and that turned me against religion. That's why I'm not a Christian."

What a cheap attitude that is! What an excuse! The only thing smarter than an excuse is a man who would try to hide behind it. But we often do blame our parents, our heredity or our environment. So what is your response? Think about it a little. You cannot live forever on pills. You cannot live on the up-rushing of your glands. You cannot live on parties, on long protracted telephone conversations and witticisms and funny remarks; think on your ways, consider your ways.

What Should Cause You to Reflect

When that soul of yours is wasted, it is gone for good. I want you to consider very carefully that your powers of moral reflection are getting weaker and weaker. Do you know what has happened in this generation? We have quenched the powers of moral reflection, even in Church circles, so that we are demanding of religious writers that they give us something condensed, brief, colorful, dramatic and full of illustrations, geared to the events and the times, which requires no thinking at all.

Today, we are demanding stories to be brief and succinct and to the point so that we can move on to something else. Moody Publishers brought out, under the editorship of Wilbur Smith, what they call the Wycliffe Series. They were the great books of the Puritan divines, but they stand on the shelves and gather dust. People are not buying them. The reason is that we have developed a mentality that simply cannot bring itself to attack a serious book. We have to be fed with an eyedropper, like a baby robin that has been pushed out of the nest in a storm. Because we feed Christians with an eyedropper, we have weaklings instead of great souls and great saints.

Consider how your power of reflection gets weaker. The little three-year-old asks more questions than the 30-year-old; and the 30-year-old asks more questions than the 50-year-old. I recommend most earnestly that you consider that your powers of moral reflection will be getting weaker and your prejudices will be getting stronger as you get older. Your habits are getting set and it will be harder to break them later on.

God patiently waits, and sometimes it seems endlessly; and then one day God says, "I accept that"; that is His response. He is saying, in effect, "They have heard the gospel and they have finally made their choice. They have settled it. They do not know it, but they have said, 'Not tonight, not now, I've got too many things to do.'" God says, "That's his response, and it's settled." There is nothing anybody can do after that.

In the face of the four last things—death, judgment, heaven and hell—consider your ways. Here we are with intelligence and ability to think and consider and reflect; the beasts that perish everywhere in all their beauty know nothing about this. God has lent you a soul for a while and says, "Reflect now, and think, and come unto Me and believe on Me and put away your sins and trust Me." What are you going to do?

When You've Truly Met God

I often wonder how much is of God and how much is merely social. I wonder if the two can be put together or if they can be interlaced so they cannot be torn apart. I wonder if the social were suddenly removed, how much of the spiritual would be left? It seems like we always have to be doing something to keep happy.

I was converted so thoroughly that I never had to be continually doing something: holding street meetings and testifying and distributing tracts and studying the Scriptures and going to another meeting and praying and doing some more praying and some more meetings. Never had to have a lot of stuff to hold me together.

Now we have to have all these things to hold our people. If we were to suddenly take them away, how many Christians would we have left out of the whole bunch? I love young people, but I am worried about them. Have they thought about their souls lately? Or are they just in the swing of a kind of religio-social stream of things?

Stop a bit. Think. Look up. Hear God speaking. Say to yourself, *Now wait a minute here, just a minute, am I really a Christian? Do I really know God? Am I really right with God? How long has it been since I've said a prayer out loud with anything but mumbling?* Ask yourself, *How long has it been since I sought God alone, with my Bible, and nobody knew it? How long since there has been a tear of repentance or joy in my eye? Am I just living on meetings and social fellowships and pizza? Or is there something more profound than that? Have I met God?*

Think on your way. I would be an evil false prophet if I did not say these things. Consider your way and let us reason together. For the dear Lord waits to do something for you and to you that will be so real, so wonderful, so transforming and revolutionary that nobody can cheat you out of it.

At 17, I met God. A year and a half later, I met Him in a mighty baptism of the Holy Spirit and fullness of the Spirit, and then I began my education. For years, I read writings on atheism and philosophical unbelief to the point that my head would ache. I would turn away and get on my knees, and with joy I would say to God, "Oh, God, I know I can't answer this man, but I thank Thee I have Thee." I would worship on my knees after having been knocked flat by a book. If I had not met God, that book would have ruined me forever.

All those books presenting atheism, unbelief, philosophy, psychology and all the books that were then current, all the debunking books and the rest, never jarred me, for I knew Jesus Christ for myself. I had seen Him, I had known Him, He deigns to walk with me, and the glory of His presence shall be mine eternally.

You can know God like that, and then you do not have to be afraid of what you learn; you do not have to be afraid of an unbelieving professor. You can stand up and face him down and say, "I cannot answer your questions, but I can tell you my testimony."

I'll Live for Him
Ralph E. Hudson (1843–1901)

My life, my love I give to Thee,
Thou Lamb of God Who died for me;
O may I ever faithful be,
My Savior and my God!

I now believe Thou dost receive,
For Thou hast died that I might live;
And now henceforth I trust in Thee,
My Savior and my God!

O Thou Who died on Calvary,
To save my soul and make me free,
I'll consecrate my life to Thee,
My Savior and my God!

I'll live for Him Who died for me,
How happy then my life shall be!
I'll live for Him Who died for me,
My Savior and my God!

15

LIVING THE DYNAMICS OF GOD'S KINGDOM

For the kingdom of God is not in word, but in power.
1 CORINTHIANS 4:20

To overcome the dangers facing a spiritually lethargic church is to discover true spiritual power. The power does not rest in outward form but rather in the dynamic of God's Word.

The apostle Paul had the authority of the chief apostle and was appointed by the Lord for several things; one was to receive and shape Church truth and lead the Church into the area of dynamic Christian living. He received the revelation directly from God. Jesus said, "I have yet many things to say unto you, but ye cannot bear them now. Howbeit when he, the Spirit of truth, is come, he will guide you into all truth: for he shall not speak of himself; but whatsoever he shall hear, that shall he speak: and he will show you things to come" (John 16:12-13).

That Spirit entered Paul when Ananias prayed for him, and he was filled with that same Holy Spirit. He received that which was behind, and he was the mold in which God poured it. Then he was also appointed by the Lord to set up a system and polity for the Church. He was appointed by the Lord to embody all authority that there was in the meantime. Perhaps most important of all, he was appointed by God to show by example the Christian way. Paul said, "I sent unto you [Timothy], who is my beloved son, and faithful in the Lord, who shall bring you into remembrance of my ways which be in Christ" (1 Cor. 4:17).

He said these things because the man of God was having his authority undercut by schismatics—men who came in and taught that Paul was not a real apostle because he never saw the Lord. The other apostles walked with Jesus while He walked among men, but they said this man Paul was not an apostle and they could prove it by the fact that he came after Jesus had died and risen. That was their argument. They overlooked the vision Paul had of Jesus, of one born out of due time (see 1 Cor. 15:8).

These schismatics and dividers of the Church had to repudiate Paul's authority in order to establish their own. They attacked Paul, but as far as Paul was personally concerned, it did not matter. He did not care: "But with me it is a very small thing that I should be judged of you, or of man's judgment: yea, I judge not mine own self" (1 Cor. 4:3). Paul knew that if he was going to have any authority, he was going to have to establish that authority. He sent Timothy to straighten them out and prepare them for his visit. Isn't it strange that there is not any thing new under the sun?

Getting to the Essence of Kingdom Power

Years ago, there was a wonderful writer for the *Chicago Daily News*. He went to see the old Greek play *Lysistrata,* and after seeing it, reported on it in his column. He wrote, "I went to see the old Greek play by Aristophanes and I came away deeply discouraged. Here is what discouraged me: not that it was not well written, not that it was not well done. But, I came away convinced that nobody had been able to think of a new joke in twenty-four hundred years. That everything old Aristophanes wrote into his funny plays is still floating all around here."

That was a worldly man talking about a worldly thing, but the same thing is true in the spiritual life. Many imagine they are original, but nobody is original except Adam. Paul wrote, "Now some are puffed up, as though I would not come to you. But I will come to you shortly, if the Lord will, and will know, not the speech of them which are puffed up, but the power. For the kingdom of God is not in word, but in power" (1 Cor. 4:18).

The Kingdom of God Is Not in Words

Here is what I want particularly to emphasize: the kingdom of God does not lie in words. I am among the few who are trying to warn the Church of this today. Not many see what the apostle Paul said back there that the kingdom of God is not in words, but in power.

Words are only the outward image of truth, and they can never be the inward essence. Words are incidental. If I were to say, "Everybody who can speak Swedish bring your New Testament next Sunday; everybody who speaks German, bring yours; Norwegian, bring yours, and so on, we would have half a dozen different languages. If I were to say, "Now read the book of Revelation," it would be quite a revelation to see that the words were only incidental. The meaning is what matters.

Somewhere in the middle of it all, there is a spiritual meaning, and the six different people have embodied that meaning in six different sets of words. Those words were not alike, or only occasionally alike. We ought to remember that. The kingdom of God is not in words. They are only incidental and can never be fundamental. When fundamentalism ceased to emphasize fundamental meanings and began emphasizing fundamental words, they shifted from meanings to words and from power to words, and they began to go downhill.

There is an essence of truth, and it may follow the form of words as the kernel in an English walnut follows the confirmation and configuration of the shell. The shell is not the kernel, and the kernel is not the shell; so while the truth follows the form of words, it sometimes deserts it. The great error is in holding the form to be the essence and putting the kingdom of God in words so that if you have got the words right, you have got the whole thing. If you can get a better set of words, you have more truth. This is not necessarily true at all.

Word and Spirit

Words deceive even good, honest Christian people who feel that there is a certain safety in mumbling words, and a power to frighten off. Tell me why the devil should be afraid of words? The devil, who is the very essence of ancient created wisdom and who had the perfection of beauty and the fullness of wisdom, and whose power lies in his shrewdness and intellectual brilliance, can you tell me how that devil should suddenly become so foolish as to be afraid of a word? Afraid of a motion? Afraid of a symbol?

I put a chain around my neck or make a motion with my fingers in front of my face to keep the devil away. I wonder what a man without any arms would do if the devil came after him and he could not make the sign of the cross. The devil is not afraid of words or symbols. You can surround yourself with religious symbols—Protestant, Catholic or Jewish—and not help yourself in the slightest, because the devil is not afraid of a symbol; he knows better.

Did you ever see the little child afraid of a mask? Put a mask on and the little child runs and yells. If the child still did that at 16, you would be ashamed of him. As soon as we grow up, we know that masks do not mean anything. Words do not mean anything, as words. We imagine that if we say certain words, they have power to bring good; if we say certain other words, they have the power to fend off the devil. That is just paganism under another form.

Paul was addressing people who recently had been pagans and only lately converted. The Greeks loved oratory and fine language, and they produced a lot of fine literature. Paul said, "For I determined not to know any thing among you, save Jesus Christ, and him crucified. And I was with you in weakness, and in fear, and in much trembling. And my speech and my preaching was not with enticing words of man's wisdom, but in demonstration of the Spirit and of power: That your faith should not stand in the wisdom of men, but in the power of God" (1 Cor. 2:2-5).

When you strip superstition away from a man, he feels terribly naked for a moment, but until we strip off our superstition the Lord cannot put on us a cloak of truth. The kingdom of God lies in power; its essence is in power. The gospel is not the statement that Christ died for our sins according to the Scriptures (see 1 Cor. 15:3). The gospel is the statement that Christ died for our sins according to the Scriptures plus the Holy Spirit in that statement, to give it meaning and power. Just the statement itself will never do it.

The Full Gospel

Have you wondered, at times, why those churches that drill their young people from childhood in the catechism and teach them the doctrines so that they are positively instructed in the Word of the truth, somehow fail to get them through to the new birth? I think it is a fine thing for young people to know doctrine. But have you noticed that there are whole generations of so-called Christians who are drilled in the catechism, who know the doctrine, who can recite the gospel as well as the law and still never manage to break through to the new birth? They never come through to that shining wonder of inward renewal.

The reason is, they are taught that the power lies in the words, and if you get the words right, you are all right. Whereas, Paul says, the kingdom of God does not lie in words at all. The kingdom of God lies in the power that indwells those words. You cannot have the power without the words, but you can have the words without the power, and many people do.

The gospel is the power of the Spirit operating through the Word. It is the statement of the fact that Christ died for our sins according to the Scriptures, that He rose again, was seen of many and that He is at the right hand of God and will forgive those who believe on Him. That is the gospel in its shell, but the power must lie in there or there will be no life in it.

The Working of the Power

Paul appealed away from man-given authority. He appealed away from speech, however eloquent, and away from even his own position. He appealed directly to the power of the risen Lord manifest through the Spirit. He said, "I want you to know, and I sent Timothy to try to straighten you out and remind you that it's the power of God that speaks, not a man's mouth." The appeal was to the power of the risen Christ. If this church and the people who composed it were not living in a constant miracle, they were not Christians at all, because the Christian life is a miracle.

It is what the ark of Noah was in the day of the Flood; it was completely separated from that flood, and yet it was floating upon it. It was what Jesus was when He walked among men; He was right in the middle of them and yet separate from sinners and higher than the highest heaven. There operates within the true Body of Christ a continual energizing by the Holy Spirit that makes a continual miracle. A Christian is not somebody who has believed only. A Christian is somebody who has believed, in power.

A Moral Power

The working of the power is a moral power. It has power to expose sin to the sinner's heart. Nobody will ever be truly saved until he knows he is a sinner, and nobody will ever know he is a sinner by simply threatening him or warning him or telling him. You can go to a man and say, "You're a sinner. You swear and lie, and you're wrong, you're evil." He will grin, shake his head and say, "I know, I shouldn't do those things, but I guess we'll all human." You have not convinced him.

You can read Plutarch, Aristotle, Herbert Spencer, Bertrand Russell and all the rest of the books of ethics and show him he is dead wrong, and he still will never know what it means to be a lost sinner. You can threaten him that if he does not look out, does not straighten out his ways, nuclear warfare will get him or terrorism will reign, and you still have not convinced him. You have not told him anything he did not know. "When he [the Holy Spirit] is come," said Jesus, "he will reprove the world of sin, and of righteousness, and of judgment" (John 16:8).

When Peter preached at Pentecost, the Scripture says, "When they heard this, they were pricked in their heart, and said unto Peter and to the rest of the apostles, Men and brethren, what shall we do?" (Acts 2:37). That word "pricked," according to Weymouth's translation, is a word stronger and deeper than the word "pierced," where they pierced the heart of Jesus with a spear. The words of Peter in the Holy Spirit, the new baptized prophet and apostle, penetrated like a spear deeper than the spear that had gone into the heart of Jesus on the cross. Forthwith came water and blood.

The Holy Spirit is not something we can argue about or somebody that we can say of, "You believe your way and I'll believe my way." The Holy Spirit is an absolute necessity in the Church. I am grieved in the Holy Spirit because there is a power in the Spirit to expose sin and revolutionize and convert and create holy men and women, and nothing else can do it. Words will not do it. Instructions will not do it. Line upon line, precept upon precept will not do it; it takes the power of God to do it.

A Persuasive Power

The working of the power is also a persuasive power to break down resistance. This is the essence of evangelism. Not arguments. Not appealing to a man's lower nature. Not even appealing to a man's intellect. Rather, it is the power of persuasion that rises above any man's ability. It is the Holy Spirit convincing a man deep in his heart that these things are true. Argument can never go that deep. Reasoning will not go that deep. Only the Holy Spirit can.

A Power that Brings Worship

Moreover, the working of the power is also a power to create reverence and excite ecstasy in true worship.

If we were to put statues all around with candles burning and beautiful Italian-made glass, colored windows, pictures of shepherds, and altars, and I were to come in a long black robe, you would have a sense of reverence. However, while I like to see beautiful windows, beautiful windows do not create it. Nor do symbols create it. Reverence is the astonished awe that comes to the human heart when it sees God. That is what the Holy Spirit can do through the Word, and nobody else can do it. I can imitate holy tones all I will, and we can try to be adjusted, religious and ecclesiastical as we can be, and still when it is all over, the feeling we get is psychological or aesthetic at best.

In 1 Corinthians 14:24-25, Paul states that when a sinner comes into a church and the power of the Holy Spirit falls upon that church, that sinner will fall on his face and say, "God is in you of a truth" (1 Cor. 14:25). So there is a power to bring reverence, to excite ecstasy, to bring worship that lies in the Word when it is given in power, and the power of the Holy Spirit is a magnetic power to draw us to Christ, and it will exalt Him above all else.

We must demand more than correct doctrine, though we dare not have less. We must have more than right living, though we dare not have less. We must demand more than a friendly atmosphere, though we dare not have less. We must demand that the Word of God be preached in power and that we hear it in power.

Paul wrote in 1 Thessalonians 1:4-5, "Knowing, brethren beloved, your election of God [and here is how I know it] . . . our Gospel came not unto you in word only, but also in power, and in the Holy Ghost, and in much assurance." That is, not only Paul had the power, but the gospel could run in power because they heard it in power. Therefore, when the Spirit of God moves through the Word preached in power and heard in power, the objectives of God are accomplished; men are made holy and sins are forgiven, and the work of redemption is done.

How can we attain to this? The old-fashioned way is prayer, faith and surrender; and I know none other. Pray; and as you pray, surrender; and as you surrender, believe. That action is for all of us. God's people have every right in the Scriptures to demand that they hear the word in power; and if they do not hear the word in power, they have a right to rise up and ask why. If you're hearing nothing but teaching, nothing but instruction; if there is no evidence of God in it, and the preacher cannot say, I appeal to God to say whether this is true or not, then you have a right to demand that somebody come that can deliver the Word in power.

On the other hand, any man who stands to preach has a right to expect that the listeners believe in power and that they are so close to God, so surrendered, so full of faith and so prayerful that the Word of God can work in power. Shall we not believe God for that kind of church? For the kingdom of God is not in words; the kingdom of God is in power.

Let us trust God for correct doctrine: we dare not have less, but we must have more. Right living? We dare not have less, but we must have more. Let us be a friendly church but beware lest it be . . . simply a friendly church. It's amazing how social-religious or religio-social atmospheres can permeate a church so that it is hard to tell which is of the Holy Spirit and which is simply nice social contacts.

I believe that both ought to be there, and I believe they can both be there. I believe that when the Early Church met and broke bread, they fulfilled both their spiritual communion and their social fellowship. So there is no reason why the two cannot be fused. There is no reason why the warm cordiality of social fellowship cannot be made incandescent with the indwelling Holy Spirit, so that when we meet and shake hands and sing and pray and talk together, we are having social fellowship plus the mighty union and communion of the Holy Spirit.

Let us be careful that it is both. To try to destroy or prevent social contact and social fellowship is to grieve the Spirit, for the Spirit made us for each other, and He meant that there should be social fellowship and friendliness together.

He meant that we should break bread, not only formally in the Church, but also in between times when we meet. He meant that we should know each other by our first names and have our social fellowships. The churches that have tried to destroy that have succeeded only in getting in a lopsided and fanatical type of church. So let us be careful lest we do not mistake the one for the other.

Let us have a friendly church. Let us have a morally right church. Let us have a church where correct doctrine is taught. But let us also have a church of which any man can come here and say, "Our gospel came not unto you in word only, but also in power, and in the Holy Ghost, and in much assurance; as ye know what manner of men we were among you for your sake" (1 Thess. 1:5).

This is most important, for the kingdom of God lies not in words, but in power.

Break Thou the Bread of Life
Mary A. Lathbury (1841–1913)

Break Thou the bread of life, dear Lord, to me,
As Thou didst break the loaves beside the sea;
Beyond the sacred page I seek Thee, Lord;
My spirit pants for Thee, O living Word!

Bless Thou the truth, dear Lord, to me, to me,
As Thou didst bless the bread by Galilee;
Then shall all bondage cease, all fetters fall;
And I shall find my peace, my all in all.

Thou art the bread of life, O Lord, to me,
Thy holy Word the truth that saveth me;
Give me to eat and live with Thee above;
Teach me to love Thy truth, for Thou art love.

O send Thy Spirit, Lord, now unto me,
That He may touch my eyes, and make me see:
Show me the truth concealed within Thy Word,
And in Thy Book revealed I see the Lord.

16

Getting Ready to Fight the Good Fight

Watch and pray, that ye enter not into temptation: the spirit indeed is willing, but the flesh is weak.

MATTHEW 26:41

On that night in the garden, the Lord Jesus Christ was about to be betrayed into the hands of sinners. He was about to offer His holy soul and have poured out upon that soul the accumulated putrefaction and moral filth of the whole race of men; and He would carry it to the tree and die there in agony and blood. I think there can be no doubt that this is the record of the most critical event in the history of the world. It had about it and upon it more mighty historic significance, greater human weight of weal and woe, than any other event or series of events in the history of mankind.

Only the one most vitally concerned anticipated this crisis and prepared for it. That man, of course, was Jesus, and He prepared for it by the most effective preparation known in heaven or in earth; namely, prayer. Our Lord prayed in the garden.

Let us not pity our Lord as some are inclined to do, but let us thank Him that He foresaw the crisis and that He went to the place of power and the source of energy and readied Himself for that event. Because He did this, He triumphantly passed the cosmic crisis before Him. I say "cosmic crisis" because it had to do with more than this world; it had to do with more than the human race; it had to do with the entire cosmos, the whole wide universe.

The Lord was dying that all things might be united in Him. That the heavens as well as the earth might be purged and that new heavens and a new earth might be established that could never pass away. All of this rested upon the shoulders of the Son of God on that night in the garden. He prepared for this cosmic event in the most effective way known under the sun, and that is by going to God in prayer.

Over against that were His disciples. They approached the crisis without anticipation; partly because they did not know, and partly because they did not care, and partly because they were too unspiritual to be concerned, and partly because they were sleepy. So, carelessly and prayerlessly and sleepily, they allowed themselves to be carried by the rolling of the wheel of time into a crisis so vital, so significant, so portentous that nothing like it has ever happened in the world and never will happen again.

They were bogged down in spiritual lethargy and were unconscious of the importance of that hour. They did not anticipate any crisis, and therefore were completely unprepared for it. The result of their failure to anticipate was that one betrayed our Lord; one denied our Lord; and all forsook our Lord and fled away. Then Christ gave them these words as a sort of a little diamond set in a great ring. He said, "Watch and pray, that ye enter not into temptation: the spirit indeed is willing, but the flesh is weak" (Matt. 26:41).

I want to point out that this prayer Jesus made that night in the garden was an anticipatory prayer; that is, He prayed in anticipation of something He knew was coming in the will of God, and He prepared for it. I want to emphasize and lay upon your conscience to practice anticipatory prayer, because battles are lost before they are fought.

Battles Are Lost Before They Are Fought

Battles are *always* lost before they are fought. You can write that line across your heart or across your memory, and the history of the world and biography will support it. It was true of France in the Second World War.

During the First World War, France's cry electrified the world: "They shall not pass!" And pass they did not. France, in her strength, rose and opposed the hordes of the Kaiser. But only 25 years later, the hordes of Hitler came down, and France surrendered almost without firing a gun. To this day, men do not know why.

Why did they lose the battle? Why did France surrender? She surrendered because between her finest hour when she cried, "They shall not pass," and her disgraceful surrender, she had politically, morally and spiritually decayed, like an old tree filled with dry rot. When the tanks of Hitler came sweeping in, France went down and has never risen since. She still manifests the same spirit in her politics and in her social life that caused her to lose the Second World War.

This is also true of professional fighters. Fighting men are said to leave their victory in the nightclub. A man, to be at his fighting peak, must take care of himself. Some fighters, after gaining world acclaim and becoming popular, start going to the nightclubs, drinking, staying up all night and sleepily loafing in the day.

Then it is time to fight again. Though they try desperately to get ready by what they call training, the nightclubs have taken too much out of them. So they go into the ring and collapse in the fifth round, and people say, "How could it be that this mighty fighter should go down so disgracefully before a man who is not even rated and was not supposed to be that good?"

He lost the fight before he went into the ring, not when they counted him out there on the floor face down and unconscious. He drank, stayed up and danced half the night or all of the night. He left his victory in the nightclub.

The Battle on a Higher Level

It was also true of Israel. In the Old Testament, when Israel went in to battle righteous and prayed-up, she never lost a battle. When she went in filled with iniquity, and prayerless, she never won a battle. She always lost her battle when she worshiped the golden calf or sat down to eat and drink and rose up to play, or when she intermarried with the nations or when she neglected the altar of Jehovah and raised up a heathen altar under some tree. It was in those times that Israel lost her battles. It was by lack of anticipation; it was before it happened that she lost.

David

Not only are battles lost before they are fought, but battles are also won before they are fought. Take David and Goliath as an example. Little David with his ruddy cheeks went out and slew the mighty, roaring, breast-beating giant, who was 11 feet tall and had a sword like a weaver's beam. Tiny, stripling David went out and with one stone laid Goliath low, and with his own great sword, which David could hardly lift, cut off Goliath's head, carried that huge head by the hair and laid it before shouting, triumphant Israel.

When did David win that battle? Was it when he walked quietly out to meet that great boasting giant? No. Let somebody else try it and the words of Goliath would have proved true: "I will give thy flesh unto the fowls of the air, and to the beasts of the field" (1 Sam. 17:44). Under other circumstances, he would have done just that.

David was a young man who knew God, had slain the lion and the bear and had taken his sheep as the very charge of the Almighty. He had prayed and meditated and lay under the stars at night and talked to God and had learned that when God sends a man, that man can conquer any enemy, no matter how strong. So it was not that morning on the plain between the two hills that David won; it was all down the years to his boyhood, when his mother taught him to pray and he learned to know God for himself.

Jacob

After 20 years of separation, Jacob was to meet his angry brother who had threatened to kill him. He had run away so that Esau could not kill him after he took his older brother's birthright, and now he was coming back. The Lord revealed that the next day they would meet there on the plain beyond the river Jabbok.

The next day they met, right on the plain, and threw themselves into each other's arms. Esau forgave Jacob, and Jacob conquered his brother's ire and murderous intent. When did he do it? Did he do it that morning when he walked out to meet his brother and crossed over the river? No, he did it the night before when he wrestled alone with his God. It was then that he prepared himself to conquer Esau. Esau, being the stocky, solemn, hairy man of the forest who had threatened that he would slay Jacob when he found him. How could Esau cancel that oath? God Almighty took it out of his heart when Jacob wrestled alone by the river. It is always so. Jacob conquered Esau not when they met, but the night before they met.

Elijah

Elijah defeated wicked Ahab, Jezebel and all the prophets of Baal and brought victory and revival to Israel. When did he do it? Did he do it that day on Mount Carmel? After Baal follow-ers had prayed all day long and leaped on the altar and cut them-selves until they were bloody, Elijah walked up at six o'clock in the evening at the time of the evening sacrifice. He prayed a lit-tle prayer. Was it a prayer that took him 20 minutes, as we some-times do in prayer meeting and shut others out? No, it was a blunt, brief little prayer of exactly 66 words in English. I would assume it was fewer words in Hebrew.

Did Elijah's prayer bring down the fire? Yes and no. Yes, be-cause if it had not been offered, there would have been no fire. No, because if Elijah had not known God all down the years and had not stood before God during the long days and months and years that preceded Carmel, that prayer would have collapsed by its own weight and they would have torn Eli-jah to pieces. So it was not on Mount Carmel that Baal was de-feated; it was on mount Gilead. Remember, it was from Gilead that Elijah came.

I always feel that I am a better man for reading this story about how that great, shaggy, hairy man dressed in the simple rustic garb of the peasant came down boldly, staring straight ahead and without any court manners or without any knowl-edge of how to talk or what to do. He walked straight in, smelling of the mountain and the field, and stood before the cowardly, hen-pecked Ahab and said, "I'm Elijah. I stand before Jehovah, and I'm here to tell you they'll be no rain until I say so." That was a dramatic, terrible and wonderful moment; but back of that were long years of standing before Jehovah. He did not know he was going to be sent to the court of Ahab, but he anticipated it through long prayers, waiting and meditating in the presence of his God.

Preparation for Crisis

There are crises that wait for us out there, as there was the crisis that faced Jesus and His disciples, and David, and Israel, and Daniel, and Elijah, and all the rest. And there are crises that wait for us. I want to name a few of them briefly.

When Facing Acute Trouble

The history of the race shows that trouble will come to all of us sometime. When sharp trouble, with its shocking, weakening sting, comes, some Christians meet it unprepared and, of course, they collapse. Is it the trouble that brings the collapse? Yes and no. The trouble brings the collapse in that they would not have collapsed without the trouble. But it is not the trouble that causes them to collapse, because if they had anticipated it and prepared for it, they would not have collapsed. As Proverbs 24:10 says, the man who goes down under trouble has little strength. His strength is small because his prayers are few and lean, but the man whose prayers are many and strong will not collapse when the trouble comes.

When Facing Temptation

Temptation often comes unexpected and subtle. It is unexpected and too subtle for the flesh, but anticipatory prayer gets the soul ready for whatever temptation there may be.

Was it the day that David walked on the rooftop that he fell into his disgraceful and tragic temptation with Bathsheba? No, it was the long gap of unrecorded time that the historians say was in between, and they do not know what David was doing. I know what David was *not* doing: he was not waiting on his God. He was not out looking at the stars and saying, "The heavens declare the glory of God" (Ps. 19:1).

Yes, he had done that, but now he was not doing it. David went down because the whole weight of his wasted weeks previous this temptation bore down upon him. Temptation cannot hurt you if you have anticipated it by prayer; but temptation will certainly trip you if you have not.

When Attacked by Satan

Satan's attacks are rarely anticipated because Satan is too shrewd to be uniform. If Satan established a pattern of attack, we would soon catch on to it.

If the devil were to act in a uniform way and his attacks came on a regular schedule, the human race would have found him out a long time ago. The poorest church member would have learned how to avoid him. Because he acts in a highly irregular way and mixes things up, his attacks are deadly if we have not the shield of faith to protect ourselves.

A baseball pitcher does not start throwing when the first inning begins and throw the same ball in the same place for nine innings. If he did, the score would be 128 to 0. What does he do? He mixes them up. The batter never knows what type of ball is going to appear. First up, then down, then in, then out, then low, then fast, then down the middle; he mixes them up. It is the absence of uniformity that makes the pitcher effective.

Do you think the devil is not as smart as some of these major league baseball pitchers? Do you think the devil does not know that the way to win over a Christian is to fool him by irregularity? His *modus operandi* is to never attack twice the same way on the same day and to keep coming in from one side, one time, another side another time.

Do you think that boxer goes in there and gets himself rigidly stereotyped? He leads with his left, he strikes with his right, he moves back two steps, he moves forward two steps. Why, the commonest stumblebum would win over a fighter like that. A fighter has to use his head. He attacks from one side, then from the other, then dashes in, then backs away, then pedals backward, then charges, then his left and right, then feint, then five steps, then duck, then weave, then bob, you know how fighters do it.

The devil will come after you today like a wild bull of Bashan, and tomorrow he will be as soft as a lamb; and the next day he will not bother you at all. Then he will fight you three days in a row, and then let you alone for three weeks. Remember what was said of Jesus after the three temptations? He left Him for a season. Why? To get the Lord to drop His guard, of course.

The devil fights like a boxer, pitches like a skilled pitcher and uses all kinds of strategy. That is why I say that it is hard to anticipate him; you do not know what he is going to do next. You can always put a blanket anticipation down by realizing that the devil is always after you; and so by prayer and watching and waiting on God, you can be ready for his coming when he does come. You can win—not the day he arrives, but the day before he arrives. Not the noon he gets to you, but the morning before the noon.

Never Let the Day Creep Up on You

The only way to win consistently is to keep the blood of the Lamb on the doorposts of your heart; to keep the cloud and fire over you in the way Jehovah God led the Israelites night and day through the desert; to keep your fighting clothes on and never allow the day to creep up on you.

Never get up late in the morning and look at your clock and say, "I'm late and can't take time now," and dash away. If you must dash away, take a New Testament along. Instead of reading a magazine or newspaper on your break or at lunch, read your New Testament, and then bow your head and talk to God. Rather than not pray at all, grab prayer somewhere. As Bishop Ralph Cushman (1879–1960) wrote in "I Met God in the Morning":

I met God in the morning
when the day was at its best,
And His Presence came like sunrise,
Like a glory in my breast.

All day long the Presence lingered,
All day long He stayed with me,
And we sailed in perfect calmness
O'er a very troubled sea.

Other ships were blown and battered,
Other ships were sore distressed,
But the winds that seemed to drive them,
Brought to me a peace and rest.

Then I thought of other mornings,
With a keen remorse of mind,
When I too had loosed the moorings,
With the presence left behind.

So, I think I know the secret,
Learned from many a troubled way:
You must seek Him in the morning
If you want Him through the day!

Never let Thursday floor you because you did not pray on Wednesday. Never let Tuesday get you down because you were prayerless on Monday. Never let three o'clock in the afternoon bring you down because you did not pray at seven o'clock in the morning. I have four recommendations to help you value the necessity and power of prayer and to stay on top of what each day brings.

Never Act as if Things Were All Right
If the devil lets you alone for a while, and you are not in much trouble and you are reasonably happy and reasonably spiritual, you are likely to develop a complex that says, "Things are all right," and you will neglect your prayer life. Remember: As long as sin and the devil, disease and death are abroad in the land like a fire, like a contagious disease, things are not all right. You are not living in a healthy or wholesome world, a helpful world, a world that is geared to keep you spiritually healthy. This vile world is not a friend of grace to lead us on to God: it is the opposite. Instead of assuming that things are all right, assume that they are always wrong, and then prayerfully prepare for them and anticipate them in whatever direction they come.

Never Trust the Devil
Do not trust the devil and say, "Things are all right, and I don't need to pray now. This devil business is overdone, and I will not pray today. I will wait until Wednesday."

You cannot trust the devil, because it is from the devil that all of the world's tyrannical and genocidal governments past and present learn their technique and get their psychology. We must *never* trust the devil. Never imagine that he is smiling; never look at a picture of him by Paul Gustave Doré, or some other artist, and say, "Oh, he's not a bad-looking devil; perhaps all this is more or less just like Santa Claus and Jack Frost; it's only imaginary."

Always anticipate any possible attack by watching and praying; for the spirit is willing, but the flesh is terribly weak.

Never Become Overconfident

Many a man has lost a fight by being overconfident. Many a businessman has lost a business because he was overconfident. Self-confidence takes our focus off Christ and puts it on ourselves and our abilities, which fall far short in comparison with the devil's. Our confidence must always be in Christ and His abilities. Whenever we think that we can, we usually end up failing miserably.

It is a wise devil that feeds into a person's confidence in self. The devil is willing to give as much credit to "self" as long as he accomplishes his objective.

Never Underestimate the Power of Prayer

"Watch and pray," said Jesus, and He practiced it; He won because He practiced prayer and caught the spinning world that sin had thrown out of gear, caught it in the web of His own love and redeemed us by the shedding of His own blood. He did it because He had prepared Himself for that awful, yet glorious, event by prayer the night before, and by prayer in the mountains at other times, and by prayer down the years through His boyhood.

Remember that without prayer, you cannot win; and with it, you cannot lose. Granted, of course, that it is true prayer, and not just the saying of words; and granted that your life is in harmony with your prayer. If you fail to pray, you cannot win. For the Lord gave us the example of anticipatory prayer—getting ready for any event by seeking the face of God in watchful prayer at regular times.

Am I a Soldier of the Cross
Isaac Watts (1674–1748)

Am I a soldier of the Cross,
A foll'wer of the Lamb,
And shall I fear to own
His cause Or blush to speak His name?

Must I be carried to the skies
On flow'ry beds of ease
While others fought to win the prize
And sailed thro' bloody seas?

Are there no foes for me to face?
Must I not stem the flood?
Is this vile world a friend to grace
To help me on to God?

Sure I must fight if I would reign;
Increase my courage, Lord!
I'll bear the toil, endure the pain,
Supported by Thy Word.

17

Living as an Intentional Christian

*Looking unto Jesus the author and finisher of our faith; who for
the joy that was set before him endured the cross, despising the shame,
and is set down at the right hand of the throne of God.*

HEBREWS 12:2

The great deterrent to victorious Christian living is the idea
that once we accept Jesus Christ as Savior and believe that John
3:16 is all there is to it, our life now is on automatic pilot and
we can just sit back and enjoy the ride. This is the source of a
great deal of disillusionment that leads to discouragement in
the Christian life.

There is no such thing as automatic pilot in our Christian
experience; every step is an operation of faith that will be
fiercely contested by the enemy of our soul. This kind of automatic pilot thinking leads to spiritual lethargy. Breaking out
from the tyranny of spiritual lethargy—whatever the cost—
should be the number-one priority of every Christian.

I have tried to lay out some guidelines in dealing with the
various aspects of spiritual lethargy, which is the primary condition among evangelicals today leading to a variety of troubles. Let me close this study with some encouraging advice for

those who would like to break out of this spiritual bondage and get into the sunshine of God's delightful glory and purpose.

Begin with Your Own Shortcomings

The first thing is to recognize the danger of spiritual lethargy. If you do not know something is dangerous, you are not going to stay away from it, nor are you going to do anything to avoid it. Your attitude will be rather careless and indifferent, which is the perfect formula for a condition of spiritual lethargy.

Make sure you start with yourself. Many find it easy to see this problem in others. In fact, most Christians are quite ingenious in recognizing these conditions in others while remaining totally oblivious to the condition in their own life. We have become experts in other people's shortcomings but quite naïve about our own personal standing with God. Jesus charged the religious leaders of His day with this very thing:

> And why beholdest thou the mote that is in thy brother's eye, but perceivest not the beam that is in thine own eye? Either how canst thou say to thy brother, Brother, let me pull out the mote that is in thine eye, when thou thyself beholdest not the beam that is in thine own eye? Thou hypocrite, cast out first the beam out of thine own eye, and then shalt thou see clearly to pull out the mote that is in thy brother's eye (Luke 6:41-42).

It is important for each of us to recognize these symptoms in our own life and then solemnly vow to do something about it. A good motto I have found in this area is, *Be easy on others but hard on yourself.* Too often, we are guilty of accepting in ourselves what we vehemently condemn in others. In this area, rely on the faithfulness of the Holy Spirit to deal with this and then allow Him to be as thorough as necessary in your life. God loves you too much to let this condition continue unchallenged.

The Holy Spirit is faithful in exposing your spiritual condition. Your responsibility is to listen to the Holy Spirit, follow through on His action and take a solemn vow to break the lethargy at all cost. Remember what Solomon said along this line: "When thou vowest a vow unto God, defer not to pay it; for he hath no pleasure in fools: pay that which thou hast vowed" (Eccles. 5:4).

Lady Julian of Norwich (ca. 1342–ca. 1416) understood this about as well as anybody I have read. She wrote, "O God, please give me three wounds; the wound of contrition and the wound of compassion and the wound of longing after God." Then she added this little postscript, which I think is one of the most beautiful things I have ever read: "This I ask without condition, Father; do what I ask and then send me the bill. Anything that it costs will be all right with me."

We of the evangelical persuasion want God to do all the work and we get an easy ride to glory. Certainly, Christ has paid the full price for our redemption, but our walk with God on a daily basis will cost us much. Are we willing, cheerfully, to pay the cost?

Do Not Forsake Gathering Together

What hinders in this process is our relationship to a Christian community. I believe everybody ought to be associated with a Christian community, but we should never allow that community to dictate our spiritual growth. It is hard for us as Americans to understand that Christianity is not a democracy. The genius of our Christian walk is our utter surrender to Jesus Christ and none other. There are times when to follow the leading of the Holy Spirit in our life we must walk alone, which goes contrary to our natural inclination. Sometimes we must walk away from the crowd, even the Christian crowd.

When the Holy Spirit begins to move in our life, we believe that we can change the Christian community. As always, it backfires on us, allowing the community to change us and set our standards. Mob psychology sometimes infests even the Christian community, which may explain all the dead churches in our country today.

You cannot change the community, which is beyond the scope of possibility, but you can change yourself. Or, rather, you can allow the Holy Spirit to change you, and that change takes place at the very core of your life. Then that inward change will slowly begin affecting the outside.

The right kind of change can affect everyone around you. This spiritual awakening is not dependent on the community, but it can drastically affect the community. The change in your life can affect change in the community. Like a fire that starts small can inflame everything around it, the fire of spiritual awakening within can flow through us and touch everyone around us, in effect, changing our community.

An Intentional and Purposeful Life

I call this influence intentional Christian living. By that, I mean we are living out the guidelines and commands of the Scripture, intentionally and purposefully. Spiritual lethargy results in a Christian lifestyle that is haphazard and lazy; our commitment as Christians is to live a lifestyle that models Christ. We are not to look like or act like other people; rather, we are to look like Christ. We are to act like Christ. We are to do the things that Christ would do in the power and demonstration of the Holy Spirit.

The intentional Christian life is powered by the Holy Spirit and motivates us into a lifestyle contrary to everything around us in our culture. We are, as a former generation taught, a separated people; we are separated from the world unto God. Several things are important in maintaining an intentional Christian lifestyle.

Faith

Faith is not some magical formula or ritual, but rather it is a result of a consistent and sacrificial commitment to Bible reading and prayer. Too many are satisfied with just a verse a day to keep the devil away. This is superstitious nonsense and needs to be put away at all cost. Nothing will ever take the place of the simple reading of God's Word, preferably on your knees. Of course, Bible reading calendars are important and certainly have their use. There are times in my Bible reading when a verse or a word monopolizes my time and it raptures me, forbidding me to go another verse. It is at times like this that I need to put away all schedules and quietly and patiently wait upon the Spirit of God as He broods over that Scripture and draws me into His sweet fellowship.

Much is being said of faith these days that is not the focus of the Scriptures. We must shun all ways contrary to Scripture. Faith is not the key to get you what you want. Faith is not some magical formula that no matter who uses it, saved or unsaved, God has to act upon it. Such is religious lunacy and borders on witchcraft. I firmly believe that true faith rises in the soul of the man or woman who will fall on his face before an open Bible and allow God to be God in his life.

Obedience and Surrender

Another aspect of the intentional Christian life is obedience. I am sure this is where many fail. In order to obey fully, you must hear the voice of God clearly. Again, this is rooted in my relationship to the Word of God. Abraham of old heard God clearly and was able to obey God fully. If we are to live a life of obedience, we must have "ears to hear."

Along with this matter of obedience is surrender. Surrender is a clear act of obedience to the Word of God. When I talk about surrender, I am talking about the idea of absolutely and completely giving over my life to God, whatever it entails, without any strings attached. Some would give God as much as 99 percent of their life, but they want to hold on to that last 1 percent. Either God is Lord of all, or He is not Lord at all. Either we have completely surrendered 100 percent of ourselves to God or we have not done anything acceptable to God. Our Father will not accept a partial surrender. He is jealous toward us—all of us.

Purity

An important aspect of intentional Christian living is purity. This purity is the absence of additives. The evangelical church has become most ingenious in this area of additives. We have so encumbered the Christian life that the average Christian is weighed down with such religious trappings they never get around to living the life Christ designed for them. Purity of life is a life free from additives. The intentional Christian life is not diluted with elements of culture or religion. The purity of our life is simply the authority of the Lord Jesus Christ Himself. No other level of purity will be accepted. As I intentionally live the Christian life, I am focused on His purity, and He is living His life through me unencumbered by other things or interests.

On the surface, this looks absolutely impossible to do. And, quite frankly, it is impossible in the flesh. The more I try to live the Christian life the more I am bogged down in exterior trappings. When I put these aside and refuse to be affected or influenced by them, I then give way for God to work through me according to His agenda and His purpose. The apostle Paul said it this way: "I am crucified with Christ: nevertheless I live; yet not I, but Christ liveth in me: and the life which I now live in the flesh I live by the faith of the Son of God, who loved me, and gave himself for me" (Gal. 2:20). It is no longer me; it is Christ in me, the hope of glory.

Enjoying God's Favor

Those of us who are utterly committed to living an intentional Christian life have one great advantage. This advantage is the way God thinks about us. God has our best in mind for the longest period of time.

What God is doing in your and my life today not only has implications for today but for all eternity. When Jesus Christ was on the cross, we were on His mind. The tears that flowed on Calvary were because of us.

The writer to the Hebrews refers to the fact that Jesus endured the cross because of the joy before Him: "Looking unto Jesus the author and finisher of our faith; who for the joy that was set before him endured the cross, despising the shame, and is set down at the right hand of the throne of God" (Heb. 12:2). What was that joy? It was all those who would put their faith and trust in Him and become part of the Bride of Christ. We are always on His mind.

God desires to bring our lives into the full sunlight of His favor. That requires not serving ourselves or pleasing others or ourselves, but giving ourselves completely, in absolute surrender, to God through the Lord Jesus Christ our Savior. The end result is living the intentional Christian life.

Yield Not to Temptation
Horatio Richmond Palmer (1834–1907)

Yield not to temptation, for yielding is sin;
Each vict'ry will help you some other to win;
Fight manfully onward, dark passions subdue;
Look ever to Jesus, He'll carry you through.

Shun evil companions, bad language disdain,
God's name hold in rev'rence, nor take it in vain;
Be thoughtful and earnest, kindhearted and true;
Look ever to Jesus, He'll carry you through.

To him that o'ercometh, God giveth a crown,
Through faith we will conquer,
    though often cast down;
He who is our Savior, our strength will renew;
Look ever to Jesus, He'll carry you through.

Ask the Savior to help you,
Comfort, strengthen, and keep you;
He is willing to aid you,
He will carry you through.

Follow Tozer's new writings on Twitter at
http://twitter.com/tozeraw

A SHORT BIOGRAPHY OF A.W. TOZER

Adapted from The Life of A. W. Tozer
by James L. Snyder

During his lifetime, many regarded A. W. Tozer as a twentieth-century prophet. Unlike many other leaders in the Church at the time, he was able to discern that modern Christianity was sailing through dense fog and could easily flounder if it continued its present course. His spiritual intuition enabled him to see error, name it for what it was and reject it—all in one decisive act. He could tear to pieces in a few short sentences the faulty arguments of others.

Aiden Wilson Tozer was born on April 21, 1897, in La Jose (now Newburg), a farming community in the hills of western Pennsylvania. His mother named him for the storekeeper husband of a close friend from childhood. He never liked his given names, preferring instead to go by the initials "A. W." In later life, he preferred just "Tozer."

Tozer's grandfather, Gilbert Tozer, emigrated from England to the United States in the mid-1800s and married Tozer's grandmother, Margaret Weaver, in 1850. The couple had eight children (four boys and four girls). Jacob Snyder Tozer, A. W. Tozer's father, was born in 1860. He married Prudence Jackson, a young girl from a nearby town who knew little of country life. They had six children, of which Aiden Wilson was the third.

Tozer grew up on a farm in rural Pennsylvania and received a limited education at Wood School, so named because of its pine woods setting. Later, during his teen years, he enrolled in a correspondence course in cartooning. Although he did not complete the course, he showed considerable promise.

In 1912, Tozer and his family moved to Akron, Ohio, a bustling city and a center for rubber production in the country. Tozer's first job was selling candy, peanuts and books as a "butcher boy" on the Vicksburg and Pacific Railroad. However, because he preferred to sit and read the books he was supposed to be selling, he made little money at it. Eventually, he found a job at Goodyear cutting chunks of crude rubber into tiny bits. Tozer worked nights, and as he did the monotonous work with his hands, he would put up a book of poetry in front of him and memorize it as he worked.

In 1915, three years after arriving in Akron, Tozer was walking home from work when he saw a man speaking to a crowd on a street corner. He was not able to hear what the man was saying, so he crossed the street and joined the crowd. At first, the man's words made little sense to Tozer (he spoke with a strong German accent), but he eventually realized that the man was preaching. At one point, the preacher said, "If you don't know how to be saved, just call on God, saying, 'God, be merciful to me, a sinner,' and God will hear you."

The words burned in Tozer's heart and awakened within him a gnawing hunger for God. When he arrived home, he went to the family attic, where he could be alone to think through what the preacher had said. When he emerged, he was a new creation in Christ Jesus. His pursuit of God had begun.

Aiden Tozer married Ada Pfautz at Grace Methodist Episcopal Church on April 26, 1918. Although his English was poor and laced with western Pennsylvania colloquialisms, he began preaching on the streets in Akron after his shift at Goodyear had concluded for the day. While his sermons were not models of good spoken English, he was beginning his ministry and gaining valuable experience.

In 1919, Robert J. Cunningham, pastor of the Stonewood Christian and Missionary Alliance Church in West Virginia, invited Tozer to come to Clarksburg for a two-week evangelistic campaign. At the conclusion of the two weeks, the congregation asked Tozer to become pastor of the church, which he accepted. This event would mark the beginning of his 44 years of affiliation with the denomination. He remained in Clarksburg for two years and then accepted a position as pastor in a larger Christian and Missionary Alliance church in Morgantown.

From Morgantown, Tozer went to the East Side Chapel of the Christian and Missionary Alliance in Toledo, Ohio, and pastored there until 1924. He continued his practice of evangelism within his community and regularly accepted invitations to preach in other churches. Summer Bible conferences were becoming popular in the denomination, and Tozer often served as a youth evangelist at these gatherings. It was in Morgantown that Ada Tozer gave birth to the couple's first three boys: Lowell, Forrest Leigh and Aiden Wilson, Jr.

In December 1924, Tozer began a four-year ministry at an Alliance church in Indianapolis, Indiana. During this time, he developed the pulpit ministry for which he later would be known and began writing for the monthly church newsletter, *The Light of Life*. In 1928, the Southside Gospel Tabernacle in Chicago, Illinois, sent several letters to Tozer inviting him to consider becoming their pastor. However, the Indianapolis church was prospering and the congregation was good to him, so Tozer simply tossed the letters in the wastebasket.

The Chicago congregation was persistent and kept sending letters to Tozer. Finally, he agreed to go to Southside Tabernacle for a Sunday and preach at the church. When it came time for him to speak, he rose from his chair and, omitting any niceties (such as being happy to be there), he announced his sermon topic: "God's Westminster Abbey." Tozer took his text from Hebrews 11, and the congregation was soon caught up in his sermon.

Tozer eventually warmed up to the idea of being the pastor at Southside Tabernacle. In a meeting with the board, he told the members that if they wanted him to serve in their church, they had to allow him to focus on preparing his sermons on Sundays. This meant certain conditions—such as reducing visitations among the congregation. After considerable discussion and prayer, the board agreed to Tozer's stipulations and issued him an official call, which Tozer accepted. He would serve at Southside Tabernacle for 31 years.

During the 1930s and 1940s, Tozer's preaching gained attention in the Chicago area because it was different. While others were offering clever outlines and meticulous word studies, Tozer led his listeners straight into an encounter with God. He studiously avoided any artificiality in his preaching or religious nonsense or trivia, focusing instead on issues of paramount spiritual importance to his listeners. Passing trends were never fodder for his contemplation, and people went away from his ministry with the haunting sense that they had just been in the immediate presence of God.

Tozer's sermons were warm and alive, and he worked hard not to be like other preachers. He did not want his sermons to *sound* like sermons, so he structured them more like magazine articles, teaching spiritual principles rather than reciting the exegesis of verses. His listeners frequently had the feeling that he was turning on a water faucet and then turning it off when there was enough. He would begin by reading his text, usually brief, and then he would say, "Now, I want to make a few remarks by way of introduction." Then, without the listener realizing how much time had slipped by, he would say, "Well, I see my time is up. I'll stop here and finish this tonight."

Sermon preparation was a constant process with Tozer. It did not matter if he was riding a streetcar or train, or if someone was driving him to an appointment across town. He would get settled in his seat and immediately take out a book. It might be a book he was reading at the time or a spiral notebook in which he would jot down sermon notes. He was constantly reading, studying, thinking and writing.

By 1939, Ada and A. W. Tozer's family included six sons. After a nine-year hiatus, the Tozers welcomed a daughter, Becky, into their home. Tozer later reflected on that momentous event in a sermon, stating, "She was a lovely little thing. After raising six boys—it was just like trying to bring up a herd of buffaloes—this refined, feminine little lady came along with all her pretty, frilly things. She and I became sweethearts from the first day I saw her little red face through the glass in the hospital. I was forty-two years old when she was born."

In 1943, Tozer wrote his first book, *Wingspread*, the biography of Albert B. Simpson, founder of the Christian and Missionary Alliance, which was Tozer's denomination. In 1946, he was elected vice president of the Christian and Missionary Alliance, a position he held for four years. In 1946 he wrote *Let My People Go*, the life story of missionary Robert A. Jaffray, who pioneered the Alliance work in Indochina and Indonesia and died in the closing days of World War II in a Japanese concentration camp. In 1948 he wrote *The Pursuit of God*, which ultimately became his best-known spiritual treatise.

In 1950, two years after *The Pursuit of God* appeared, Tozer was named the editor of the *Alliance Weekly*, the denominational publication of the Christian and Missionary Alliance. That same year he wrote *The Divine Conquest*, in which he challenged believers in Christ to allow the Holy Spirit to cross the threshold of their personality and inspire their souls. In 1953, he followed this work with *Born After Midnight*, a collection of editorials he had written for *Alliance Life*.

In 1954, Tozer's first term as editor of *Alliance Life* ended and, to the shock of the denomination, he submitted his resignation. Despite this fact, when the church council convened that same year, Tozer allowed himself to be reelected. Under Tozer's leadership, the magazine's circulation doubled, and he remained the editor for the publication until his death. More than any single entity, *Alliance Life* established Tozer as a spokesperson for the Christian and Missionary Alliance and the evangelical church at large. His readership was larger outside his denomination by a wide margin.

In 1955, Tozer published *The Root of the Righteous*, a collection of his earlier *Alliance Life* editorials. This was followed in 1957 by *Keys to the Deeper Life*, a series of articles that Tozer wrote for a Christian magazine. In 1958, *The Alliance Weekly* became *The Alliance Witness*, which in turn became *Alliance Life* in 1987.

By the late 1950s, the neighborhood around the Southside Alliance Church had deteriorated to the point where the board felt it was necessary to make a move. Tozer agreed that relocation was the only solution, but he did not agree that he should lead such a migration. He had been through one building program 22 years earlier, and at age 62 he did not relish the responsibility of another. So, on June 27, 1959, he resigned as pastor.

Shortly afterward, the Avenue Road Church in Toronto, Canada, asked Tozer to serve as its pastor. Tozer at first refused, but he later accepted an offer by the church superintendent to preach twice each Sunday and allow a younger pastor to handle all of the other church responsibilities. In doing so, Tozer agreed to be the teaching pastor at the church for a "few months"—a term that eventually extended to four years.

In 1960, Tozer published *Of God and Men*, the third and final collection of his editorials from *Alliance Life*. He followed this in 1961 with *The Knowledge of the Holy*, a study of the attributes of God that many consider to be his crowning literary achievement. He also completed *The Christian Book of Mystical Verse*, a compilation of the writings of many of the saints that he admired. He looked forward to writing one more book on worship, but did not live long enough to finish the project.

In the summer of 1962, Tozer returned briefly to Chicago for the denominational Life Investment Conference, where he preached to 1,200 youth from across North America. In May 1963, Tozer experienced some chest pain. His condition improved quickly and he looked forward to being discharged Sunday, May 12, in time to preach the Sunday evening sermon at the Alliance General Council on May 19. That evening, Ada arrived at the hospital to visit him, and she kissed him goodnight for the last time at 10:00.

An hour later, a nurse went in to check on Tozer and discovered that he was having another heart attack. Staff efforts to stabilize his condition were not successful, and shortly after midnight, on Sunday, May 12, 1963—not quite a week after preaching his last sermon—Aiden Wilson Tozer found himself "away from the body and at home with the Lord." He was buried in Ellet cemetery in Akron, Ohio, with a simple epitaph marking his grave: "A. W. Tozer—A Man of God."

A.W. TOZER:
THE AUTHORIZED BIOGRAPHY

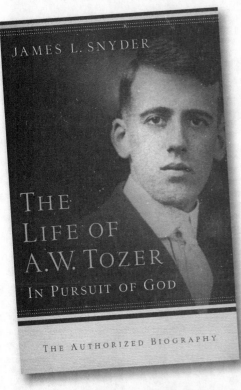

THE LIFE OF A.W. TOZER
IN PURSUIT OF GOD
James L. Snyder
ISBN 978.08307.46941
ISBN 08307.46943

To understand the ministry of A.W. Tozer, it is important to know who he was, including his relationship with God. In *The Life of A.W. Tozer*, James L. Snyder lets us in on the life and times of a deep thinker who was not afraid to "tell it like it is" and never compromised his beliefs. A.W. Tozer's spiritual legacy continues today as his writings challenge readers to a deeper relationship and worship of God in reverence and adoration. Here is Tozer's life story, from boyhood to his conversion at the age of 17, to his years of pastoring and writing more than 40 books (at least two of which are regarded as Christian classics and continue to appear on bestseller lists today). Examining Tozer's life will allow you to learn from a prophet who had much to say against the compromises he observed in contemporary Christian living and the hope he found in his incredible God.

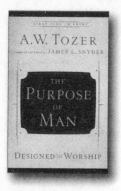

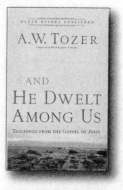
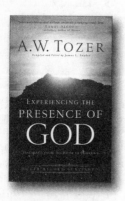
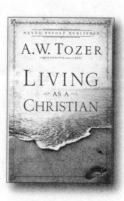
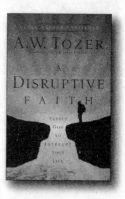

DISCOVER THE CLASSIC WRITER WHO IS STILL CHANGING LIVES TODAY

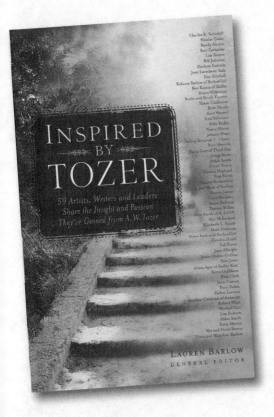

INSPIRED BY TOZER
Lauren Barlow, General Editor
ISBN 978.08307.59293
ISBN 08307.59298

A. W. Tozer lived and wrote a century ago, casting a vision of authentic faith and passionate worship that has taken root in the hearts of each new generation, including young Christ-followers today. In *Inspired by Tozer*, Lauren Barlow, drummer and singer for the award-winning pop group Barlow Girl, has assembled a diverse team of people who, like her, have been inspired by Tozer. Each contributor draws upon a Tozer quote, concept or challenge, and then shares his or her insights, challenging you to move to a deeper place of worship and holy living. These readings will introduce you to one of the Church's most treasured teachers and draw you into a relentless pursuit of God.

INCLUDES ORIGINAL, NEVER BEFORE PUBLISHED WRITINGS BY A. W. TOZER